THE ANCIENT MIND
AND ITS HERITAGE

By Elmer G. Suhr

VENUS DE MILO—THE SPINNER
THE ANCIENT MIND AND ITS HERITAGE

THE ANCIENT MIND
AND ITS HERITAGE

VOLUME I

EXPLORING THE PRIMITIVE, EGYPTIAN
AND MESOPOTAMIAN CULTURES

BY ELMER G. SUHR

FOREWORD BY PROFESSOR VAN L. JOHNSON
Department of Classics
Tufts University

AN EXPOSITION–UNIVERSITY BOOK

EXPOSITION PRESS   NEW YORK

EXPOSITION PRESS INC., 386 Fourth Avenue, New York 16, N.Y.

FIRST EDITION

To

RICHARD EUGENE HAYMAKER

amicitiae causa

FOREWORD

THE BEST HISTORICAL TRADITION has always been concerned with those involved relationships which exist between man on the one side and his universe on the other. From Herodotus to Gibbon the emphasis lay on man as the maker of his history: for the most part, history was explained as the complicated emanation of human thoughts, emotions, and activities. Since Maine and Buckle at least, the historian's outlook has been somewhat reversed, largely under the influence of Darwin and his accepted theories of man's biological development. Just within the past century, history has become a science with special techniques for the examination of source material and for the establishment of inductive generalizations based upon such evidence.

This no doubt gives us more certainty in our efforts to reconstruct the past, but it has its limitations: the procedures involved lead necessarily to a concentration on origins, rather than on ends or purposes or on the motivation of human endeavor. History, as an art, erred perhaps in the opposite direction: Clio was one of the Muses and she often charmed her devotees into pleasant fabrications of motive, word, or even deed which imagination, truthful or erroneous, supplied to fill artistic uses. But something is lost when the Muses come down from Helicon; and Clio in secular garb looks pretty drab, in secular voice, sounds pretty dull. The gifted historian will always strive to recapture some of her ancient grace. This, I think, Professor Suhr has sought to do in the volume before us, and both his intent and his achievement are highly laudable.

It is no easy task to satisfy the claims of history when we recognize this double aspect of their sanction; but an art historian like Professor Suhr has a certain initial advantage in understanding how to gratify the rules of art and how to meet the needs of science. In a work of such great scope the author has wisely relied upon expert opinion in the various divisions of his subject, and his correlation of facts rests firmly on his own vast knowledge of art objects which, like music, address all people—so to speak—in the same language.

But in addition, Professor Suhr retains the instincts of a Classical scholar, always aware of humanity itself, whether this lodges with an individual or with a type or with that paradox of modern reasoning, generic individuality as represented by the "democratic man." A single image from the manuscript of Professor Suhr's book keeps returning to me—that of man upright on a plane of infinite experience. He is not crawling on all fours or behaving merely as an animal reacting to given conditions in his environment or his inheritance. He faces the universe erect and well-furnished by nature for a great adventure of self with unself.

PROFESSOR VAN L. JOHNSON
Department of Classics
Tufts University, Medford, Mass.

PREFACE

THIS STUDY IS AN ATTEMPT to examine and evaluate the viewpoints of ancient peoples, especially those which have contributed to the development of thought in the West. It probes into the reasons why ancient peoples looked at their world and fellow men as they did, and studies what each one added and in what ways each one retarded the advance toward the democratic view of life.

What do we mean by the democratic view of life? Democracy is far from being an elixir stored up in a written document or in the mind of a political theorist; it springs from a view of life and the world, a view that creates as by-products such assets as our Constitution, the Bill of Rights, the right of universal suffrage, freedom of speech and the right to a fair trial. The mere form of a democratic government may harbor—even protect—an ever-increasing undesirable element long before the superstructure collapses in favor of some form of absolutism or anarchy. Democracy is more than middle-class respectability, more than voting and paying taxes, more than shining up the mirror of self-perfection; it is a program in which each one must contribute effort, in terms of thought and action, for the benefit of the society and government of which the individual and citizen is a part—a perennial shareholder instead of a tiny unit looking dimly through a telescope at a monstrous ogre.

In terms of thought, the thinking subject must be ready to vest the object with dignity, in order to create and maintain a fair balance between subject and object, whether the latter is a rubber ball, the family cow or the pilot of a flying saucer. If the object is brought down to a lower scale of values, the subject is resorting to a philosophy of expediency that allows an object to become a means to a personal end, thus robbing the latter of its self-respect. This is the method of the primitive magician, the scheming politician, the high-powered salesman and the court historian. A problem constitutes a conflict between the subject and object, man and circumstances, or between what I want and what the object can or will give, and a problem can only be dealt with fairly by treating the other party with the utmost fairness. The game of snap-the-whip is a legitimate activity on the playground but a boomerang in the broader sphere of human affairs.

The world in which the democratic man lives must be potential in nature, not divided between absolutes—a world where things and men are not to be separated into pallid purity and naughty black, into negative goodness and nasty evil; it must be open to improvement or deterioration at the hands of the thinking and acting man. And as the agent exerts himself in either direction, not only will his world become better or worse, but man too will improve or degrade himself. This position of a potential man in the center of a potential universe lays a heavy weight of responsibility on the shoulders of the subject, who must either face up squarely to the role or retreat to the level of a tool in the hands of a coddling but cleverly unscrupulous superior. Once potentiality fades from man's perspective, once he shirks his duty toward the needs around him, he will easily fall victim to dictatorship or to another form of absolute authority always ready to rob him of his right of decision in favor of a shallow, deceptive security.

And security can be most appealing to one who grows weary of human weakness, the stubborn face of circumstance and the misfortune and tragedy that often lie in wait for individual initiative. The Spanish castle, the El Dorado of our dreams, the novel of escape, the political utopia, the stereoscopic clarity and stillness of a wax museum invite us to enter the pearly gates of a golden age; there we may remove the burden of care and problem and surrender our birthright to an apathy as vacant as the mirror's stare. Eventually comes the realization, frequently too late, that we must move either up or downstream, that drifting and dreaming soften the marrow of defiance for the digestion of the despot.

Democracy also calls for a tolerance born of a historical perspective stretching out over a horizontal plane of experience. Difference of opinion, dress or language is never a sound reason for enmity, except where one man stands on the exclusive pedestal of perfection, looking down at sordid slavery below. Tolerance also dictates that example is the most forceful and persuasive means of converting others to our way of life. The work of Francis of Assisi, Abraham Lincoln and Albert Schweitzer means more than the zeal of all the fanatics in history's annals, more than the selfish piety of thousands so good they are almost good for nothing. The awareness of human needs, mental and physical, is a perpetual reminder that goodness is not my family's jewel, my religion's reward or my nation's *gloire et victoire*, but a source of satisfaction to one who dispenses it where it is good *for* something—for the alleviation of misery, for the increase of a mutual faith in humanity.

The democratic citizen will choose, as J. Edgar Hoover has put it, self-discipline in place of self-indulgence and will place his center of responsibility in himself without expecting too much forgiveness for his wrongdoing. He will be able to face and talk to himself, free of blindfolds or opiates, knowing full well that no creature is more open to self-deception than a featherless biped.

A sense of humor is another necessary feature in the program of democracy to compensate for the responsibilities of the conscientious citizen. It implies the ability to laugh at another and at the same time to laugh at one's ridiculous self, to use another as a mirror for one's own imperfections. Humor that transcends mockery and bitter satire preserves our humility in the face of natural pride; it helps us to share and appreciate our common heritage of both strength and weakness. Rather than a token of complacency or a certification for self-perfection, it can be a saving grace of self-criticism that bodes no ill to friend or foe.

The democratic viewpoint promises freedom, but not for

the mere asking; freedom comes, like so many of the most precious values, as a by-product of sincere effort in thought and action. If we can take joy in the responsibilities of sharing, the privileges will come without restraint. Equipped with such a view on life, a group of citizens will not only create but maintain those democratic institutions we hold so sacred. To present a people like the Cubans with the pattern of democracy before they can appreciate the value of such a pattern is to hitch a spirited horse to the rear of a wagon. Integrated with the personality, encouraged by example and a broad education the democratic view of life will eventually reduce the concatenation of the law with its protective wall of police to a minimum and increase a high form of freedom for the responsible individual in a potential world.

I sincerely hope this study will make a contribution to what G. W. Allport (*Becoming,* Yale University Press, 1955, p. 100) calls "a picture of man capable of creating or living in a democracy."

For reading the chapter on "The Primitive," thanks are due Professor Angelo Anastasio of Reed College and my colleague Professor Vincent Nowlis and Professor Launor Carter for valuable suggestions; for reading the chapter on "The Egyptian" thanks are due Professor John A. Wilson; for reading "The Mesopotamian" thanks are due Professor Thorkild Jacobsen; for reading "The Hebrew" thanks are due Professor Raymond A. Bowman; and for reading "The Hindu" thanks are due Professor G. V. Bobrinskoy, all of the University of Chicago. Grateful acknowledgment is also extended to Professor H. N. Sinha of Agra College, India, for his comments on the Hindu viewpoint. Finally, thanks are due to Emeritus Professor Robert A. MacLean of the University of Rochester for his helpful criticisms on the Greek viewpoint and to Miss Maxine Fedder for her kind services in the library of the University of Chicago.

ELMER G. SUHR

University of Rochester
January, 1959

CONTENTS

THE ANCIENT MIND
AND ITS HERITAGE

INTRODUCTION

WHAT IS A PERSONALITY? Is it merely a relative manifestation on the periphery of human experience or a recent scientific discovery of something common to man from the dawn of consciousness? For the Roman, the *persona* was the actor's mask, an object through which sound could pass; the Church Fathers attached it to the members of the trinity; thence it passed into the writings of Boethius and Aquinas, and on to the philosopher of modern times, from whom the psychologist and anthropologist have inherited it. And here we have one of their definitions: "an internal organization of emotions, attitudes, idea patterns, and tendencies to overt action."[1] We must add that, from the standpoint of the ego itself, personality implies a certain self-consciousness, an awareness of one's own importance as a subjective center, traits which manifested themselves, during the Renaissance, in an emphasis on the personal pronoun and in an increased interest in biography and autobiography. One may study the personality as a whole or, using the method of differential psychology, in terms of its attributes or functions.[2]

The second of these methods can hardly be effective in the study of ancient man, because, in the first place, we cannot call any such subject into an experimental laboratory. Furthermore, whatever we may say about ancient man as a whole, the adjustment between him and his environment was different from that of modern man, and hence his outlook on the world at large and society was different. And while ancient man was just as

1. J. Gillin: *The Ways of Men*, New York, 1948, p. 573.
2. E. Fromm: *Man for Himself*, New York, 1947, p. 31; H. A. Murray & Clyde Kluckhohn: *Personality*, New York, 1949, pp. 3–5. The latter explains some of the difficulties in the study of personality.

much, if not more, an egoist as the modern, he was not in the habit of airing his personal preferences and prejudices to the same extent. To select a single character like Khufu, Akhenaton, Pericles or Cato for such a study would produce a warped conception of personality in general, even if projected into their respective times. We are reduced, then, to an attempt to resurrect an average personality for each culture or period in a given culture, in the light of its religion, history, literature and art, all of which can contribute to his general viewpoint, or we may use certain well-known personalities as symbols of their respective periods. Each one of the fields of expression in a culture will yield some information about a compromise man has effected, in terms of thought and action, between himself and his world and so will tell us something about the personality in question.

No sharp distinction can be made between heredity and environment, or, as it is also known, between nature and nurture. "The separation of heredity and environment is thus an error for which there is no excuse. . . . The developing organism is a function of the relation between the protoplasm and its environment and not strictly speaking of the one or of the other." [3] When we speak of human nature itself, or nature in terms of emotions, instincts, habits, or behavior, we think of them as the product of heredity through a long biological and psychological history as well as of cultural environment. The latter has a subtle way of merging with so-called heredity in the course of time. We must also bear in mind that because of this complexity of interwoven hereditary and environmental influences, which is unique in every individual, men have never been and never will be potentially or actually the same in the expression of thought

---

3. M. H. Krout: *Major Aspects of Personality*, Chicago, 1933, p. 82. Much the same may be said about genius. Cf. A. L. Kroeber: *Anthropology*, New York, 1948 (revised), p. 340. G. M. A. Hanfmann: *Observations on Roman Portraiture*, Collection Latonius, XI, 1953, pp. 33ff. gives some interesting suggestions for probing into the personality of the ancients, but he seems to be concerned, for the most part with how the observer viewed a personality, not so much with how the latter looked out on his world.

and action. Between certain groups and nations, of course, who have lived over an extended period in the same environment and under the influence of similar mores, the group differences may be so marked that the individual differences within the group will appear much less marked in comparison. Furthermore, because every culture tends to pass through a series of stages in the course of its history, this does not preclude general differences between groups and nations. The viewpoint of Solon in Athens was far different from that of Khufu in the old kingdom of Egypt, and since the dawn of national consciousness, the general viewpoint of the French has been different from that of the English.

If we cannot apply the psychological method to the study of ancient personality, what can we use as a basis for such a study? What can we set down as the common denominator of ancient and present-day personality?

I think we can take for granted that the ego, or self, was, as it is now, the center of all human expression; *i.e.*, the self was the point of departure for all interests, motives, values, sentiments, desires, even complexes, although the degree of consciousness associated with the self varied considerably from one period to the other.[4] For this reason, no doubt, no one in ancient times emphasized the importance of selfishness in all thought and action; it was merely taken for granted. Not until the days of Plotinus and the Church Fathers of western Europe was unselfishness stressed as a motive, and consequently selfishness received enough attention to be branded as evil. No psychologist of today will give any quarter to unselfishness in the circle of human endeavor.[5] We may very easily identify ourselves with

---

4. C. R. Knight: *Prehistoric Man*, New York, 1949, p. 69.

5. Cf. Erich Fromm: *op. cit.*, p. 131. To make a distinction between selfishness and self-love, which have much the same meaning, merely multiplies terms unnecessarily and thereby confuses the issue. In my opinion, it is much more convenient to ascribe all human effort to selfishness without applying the tarnish of a Calvin to the term; by throwing unselfishness into the discard one can make a more practical distinction between a constructive and a destructive selfishness. Cf. also my *Theme and Variations*, Boston, 1944, pp. 139ff.

God, the sufferings of our fellow man, the helplessness of the dumb brute—all of which may lead us to believe in self-sacrifice transcending human desire; ideals of altruism and self-denial, which appear to contradict basic human motives, will, when viewed over a broader historical perspective, reveal the human heart as fundamentally selfish. The only truly unselfish man, whether in ancient or modern times, is a dead one.

In spite of all our investigations in psychology, the core of personality still remains a mystery, and every textbook on the subject is no more than an attempt to see the whole in terms of its countless myriads of expression. For a long time personality lay neglected on the reference shelf of the specialist, because one cannot experiment with it in terms of the common stimulus-response method, and it cannot be ferreted out effectively by reference to a catalog of neatly arranged traits. We can only study the core of personality, as we learn from the light of the sun, by examining its reflections. Especially is this true of the past, for the personality has passed from the scene. The ego, like a gold-tainted Midas, paints its picture on all things it touches, on every thought and belief, in art, literature and history— wherever Narcissus can behold his image in the boldest relief and gayest colors. Every striving of a healthy personality is an attempt to achieve self-glorification, and if the drive is sufficiently strong and attractive in its expression, others too will identify themselves with the aims of the man and enjoy basking in his glory. The man who can expand his interests over the broadest horizon, who can identify himself with the most varied experience—in short, the man who can paint his image most vividly on his surroundings is the greatest personality. Such a man may rise above the codes of good and evil; like so many gods, he allows his followers to justify his ways to posterity.

We sometimes refer to this exceptional personality as a genius, that product of the human race whom we minimize, even vilify or exaggerate according to the clarity of the mirror he provides for our self-perfection. What is genius? For some, it is a naturally happy freak of nature; for Carlyle it was the man who works with the greatest pains; for Napoleon it was himself; for some it is a matter of overcoming obstacles in experience or personal defects,[6] and for others it is the result of ill health or neurosis. The detection of genius is, in one respect, more easy and, again, more difficult in ancient times than in modern times: there were no fond parents or friends to warp our investigations with their wishful thinking, but today there are books and teachers aplenty who revel in the precociousness of every great man's childhood. All kinds of conclusions have been drawn from the deformities of Akhenaton, the epilepsy of St. Paul, the *mission* of Christ and the *daimon* of Socrates. The sober psychologist says: "Genius might well be defined as the possession of great mental capacity together with a special ability." [7] Since most of our exceptional men come from superior families, it seems that heredity plays a weightier role than other factors in producing genius, and we may safely assume the same was true in ancient times. We must remember, however, that we are not too concerned with genius as such, except as another manifestation of a personality in the given period of a certain culture.

And how, we may ask, has a man or woman been able consciously to make his personal influence more effective? Has he directed his course along a straight and narrow pathway, or has he scattered his aims over a broad circumference of thought or action? If we glance through the pages of ancient history we shall find that the answer to this question depends on whether religion or knowledge in terms of experience is the *terminus ante quem* of his pursuits. If inspired by belief or religious enthusiasm, the individual tends to sacrifice everything to a single goal in life. St. Paul tells us very directly: "This one thing I do. . . . I press toward the mark for the prize of the high calling of God in Christ Jesus." [8] On the other hand, Socrates, in the famous prayer of the *Phaedrus*, says: "May I consider the wise man rich." [9] One would hardly contend that Aristotle, whose curiosity led him into every field of human endeavor,

---

6. E. Friedell: *A Cultural History of the Modern Age* (trans. by C. F. Atkinson), New York, 1930, Vol. I, p. 62.

7. H. A. Carroll: *Genius in the Making*, New York, 1940, p. 290.

8. Philippians 3:13–14.

9. Plato: *Phaedrus*, 279c.

followed a single star, like Moses, who was bent solely on leading his people to the Promised Land. Some men attracted followers by what we call personal magnetism, while others depended on the flow of reason and the carefulness of their thinking; some were especially attractive to their contemporaries, whiles others waited to shed a brighter light on posterity. All of them, however, were men of dynamic energy, whether meeting a specific need of their times or working for a harvest in the distant future. They summed up truth in such general terms others could easily identify themselves with it.

One may also say there are two selves in every personality: the natural beast without tradition or convention, expressing itself in uncompromisingly selfish desire, and the other self we hope, think, or believe we are. The latter is meant for the other fellow to see; it tones down or rationalizes the desires of the natural man; it may even deceive us into believing that the two selves are one and the same, namely what we want to be at our best. Such a self can make us very uncomfortable at times: it will make us attend a family reunion when we actually see no point in it; it tells us to be nice to people we dislike; it makes us ashamed, embarrassed in the presence of others; under its pressure we hesitate or doubt, become snobs or introverts, and yet we cannot dispense with it. Today we look ahead to a time when we shall bring these two selves to some kind of agreement and so achieve a healthy self-realization. In ancient times men were not aware of such a division, because self-consciousness had not yet been developed as it is today; nevertheless, they knew how to use the outer frontier as a disguise.

The ancient personality was also more impressed with the importance of physical embellishment than his modern successor.[10] "Psychologically clothing is an extension of the personality: it is part of the *persona* or mask with which one impresses others." [11] Since there was not the same wide gap between the physical and spiritual as in our Puritan, neither men

---

10. Cf. M. B. Greenbie: *Personality,* New York, 1932, pp. 82ff.

11. C. R. Aldrich: *The Primitive Mind and Modern Civilization,* New York, 1931, p. 121.

nor women had any scruples about using cosmetics for personal adornment, a conclusion for which the tombs of all ancient peoples furnish ample evidence. Compared to the Orientals and the Romans, we are naïve in this respect, and one can be quite certain that no modern lady is as well equipped in cosmetics or as skillful in their application as Nefertiti or Cleopatra.

We are not so much interested in such manifestations, however, as we are in the viewpoint of the average personality. What is meant by such a viewpoint? Perhaps it can be best illustrated by a channel into which is poured all the traditions of a cultural pattern; in the lifetime of an individual all this is synthesized and refined in one way or another before it is poured out again into his own stream of thought and action. Though it is not always easy to distinguish, in ancient times, between the ingoing and out-going streams, we may be sure that every personality put its own stamp on its current of expression. Every man saw himself as a unit in a complicated and sometimes dangerous world which threatened him at every turn. These two factors, man and his world, were always there, and to deal more effectively with such a recalcitrant object man invented tools, techniques, arts, ideas, theories, customs, beliefs—all of which wove themselves into a cultural pattern we may study with profit. One man after another grew into the pattern, and as he grew he perhaps found it necessary to expand its limitations in making his own contribution. As time went on the pattern tended to crystallize until a single man was no longer strong enough either to remold it or to make a dent in its surface. The crust of civilization, as it lay heavily on his back, sapped up his energy and a progressive personality, like Akhenaton or Pelagius, was unable to make a lasting impression. Cultures were at times contemporaneous; at times they followed one another. But the contributions of each one, far from being wasted, were absorbed by the succeeding ones in which new personalities recast them into a new mold.

The history of a personality begins, according to the psychologist, in the prenatal stage, before the child comes to grips with the world outside. In the mother's womb the embryo is supposedly free of the feeling of abject helplessness which follows the violent upset of birth, for in the womb the mother supplies its every need. Birth represents a sudden disruption of this peaceful state by exposing the child to variations of light and temperature, to the experience of breathing and a new way of acquiring food. Instinctive operations are brought into play at once to ease this difficult transition, but they by no means fill all the demands of the new adjustment. A number of authorities, including Freud, point to certain phylogenetic acquisitions inherited from earlier generations, all of which, if something more definite were known about them, would throw some light on the personality of ancient times. Whatever may have been the role of such influences, it is difficult to regard them as the predominant factors in the development of personality. The role of the concept of incest, so characteristic of primitive tribes and European peoples, has never, from the standpoint of psychology, been satisfactorily explained, but we can safely state that, for the sociologist, it serves to define and delimit the role of the individual in the group.

Returning to the child at birth, we find reality presenting itself as a very complex problem. The organism, a bundle of demanding desires, reaches out on all sides to satisfy its needs; every contact with the resistance of its environment is a blow against its self-sufficiency. The education of the child is a slow and painful process in which the ego is forced to make constant concessions to adjust itself to the other members of the family and the world outside. Desire is direct and uncompromising; it takes for granted the attainment of every end. When frustrated, the child kicks and cries before submitting to a compromise, and many such frustrations can leave behind a latent impression in the dark region of the unconscious, where it may bear fruit later in life. The outside world, as the child soon learns, is not so easily handled unless one is patient enough to build up a learning process. In practice he builds up techniques to supply his immediate needs; he learns how to appeal to the emotions of his elders, and later he weaves theories to prepare in the mind what he hopes to carry out in practice. The adult realizes he cannot extract any values from his environment unless by way of limitations, and therefore he builds up categories and patterns of these limitations, the sum of which grows into the structure of the mind. There is also a fundamental difference, one which early man could not very well appreciate, between the inner world and its desires and the world beyond: the fact that the former is monistic, unwilling to submit to a compromise, while the latter is pluralistic and therefore, as far as man is concerned, operates on different principles, constitutes the beginning of a long series of problems running throughout life.

To satisfy his fears and desires man creates a religion, sometimes also a theology, to serve as a bulwark against the unpredictability of life, the enigma of death and the vacuum which apparently looms beyond death. He organizes theories of conduct into systems of morality and law to get along better with his fellow man. He sets up a rigid control over the primitive urges of his nature and channels them into approved avenues of expression. Tribes of primitive men band together to form a kind of government for internal harmony and protection against the common enemy, a plan by which privileges and responsibilities are distributed first according to power and later, more equally and according to ability. Man's curiosity about the ultimates of existence, the mystery of his origin and destiny, the relation of man to his world are eventually aired in terms of speculative thought. All these creations on the part of man constitute compromises between what he, as a subject, desires and what he may have from objective experience, between his craving for certainty and security and the fickle uncertainty of circumstances. As the subject wrestles with the world outside he also builds up the mind as a convenient tool for dealing with future problems, and much depends on the use he makes of the mind: he may consider it as a convenient means for the self-justification of his desires or as a mirror in which, by way of comparison with the objective, he may see his own imperfections, the narrow vision of his own desires, and so learn to live more in harmony with a broader area of experience.

In a world of constant change, ancient man's most fundamental desire was for security and certainty. On the plane of
practice, he did his utmost to guarantee a lasting supply of food
and drink for his body; he also demanded a roof over his head.
On the level of religion, he tended to create a god in his own image and made himself subservient to the god's will; if successful,
such a religion, since it answered every question after a fashion,
rendered philosophy and science superfluous. An absolute form
of government, which offered a measure of security to the same
degree as it stifled exploration, was imposed on a group from
above. Knowledge stemming from conviction issued from
authority in the form of revelation; conduct was governed by
principles of the same nature. The mind, at this stage, became a
transparent glass through which the desires of man were projected and justified in terms of stereotyped truth that admits of
but few exceptions. "One's attempt to be a personality is, in
some measure, an attempt to make the world share one's own
deluded vision of the incomparable self." [12] On the other hand,
if the mind was granted the privilege of drawing in bolder
relief the impressions of that pluralistic universe beyond the
grasp of the subject, a better balance could be constructed, as
we shall see, between the subjective and objective and a better
awareness cultivated for comparative values.

On every side man found himself reaching out for the
infinite, the eternal which he believed would protect him against
the threat of change, but he learned too that it tended to clash
with the finite relationships of his experience. Today we can
allow neither a Zeno nor a Kant to play loosely with such
contradictions in the form of antinomies; the paradoxes are still
with us and present the same challenge they posed for the
Greeks and the early Chinese, but they need not be a stumbling
block. The attributes of infinity are implicit in the world beyond
our horizon: if it were possible for an aviator to fly to the outer
wall of the universe, would he rest content to have discovered
such a limitation? Hardly! His second trip would find him

---

12. M. B. Greenbie: *op. cit.*, p. 180.

equipped with appropriate tools and weapons to pierce this wall and then, like the chick in the egg shell, to learn what lies beyond this barrier. The same curiosity goads the mind to penetrate beyond the limitations of time; the more the historian, the anthropologist, and the archaeologist limit the time span of our past, the more anxious we become to use this limit as a new point of departure. Moving from the macrocosm to the microcosm, there is as much mystery and infinity in the inner man, in the microscopic entity, as in the world at large. The latter is projected by human desire into a finite realm, where it meets with all kinds of opposition.

What do we know about the origin of such a conflict or the push that causes the physical organism to function and grow in experience? The unconscious, we are told by the psychologist, is totally without any awareness of time and space relationships.[13] It is governed by the prospect of pleasure or pain. On either side of consciousness, within and without, lies an uncertain, yawning abyss whose depths our probing has failed to fathom, and between these two has grown up the mind, the agent designed to mediate between the two unknowns.

And what is the value of such an agent? What do we mean when we say "I know" or "I think I know"? The mind is a window through which the curiosity of man can derive some meaning from the world at large, and if the information thus obtained is carefully weighed, this same mind can set up a proper balance between the subject and object, without which there can be no sound thinking; it furnishes a fair compromise between what man wants and what he may have. Between Faust dedicated to magic on the one side, and Faust, the learned sceptic, on the other, the mind must make its choice and take the consequences. Once this opportunity to effect a fair compromise is lost sight of, we shall eventually lose our dignity as individuals—and perhaps even ourselves.

---

13. "The unconscious is quite timeless and the word 'no' has no significance for it (quoted from Ernest Jones)." Healy, Bronner, and Bowers: *The Structure and Meaning of Psychoanalysis*, New York, 1930, p. 23.

THE PRIMITIVE

PRIMITIVE MAN FACED THE WORLD around him without the aid of the developed reasoning and scientific inventions we have inherited from a civilized past. For this reason he was hardly as conscious as we are of himself and his world as the two great factors of human experience. But, at all events, he was forced to effect some manner of compromise between these factors if he was to survive. And because his body made certain immediate demands and his world was fraught with so many dangers to his physical well-being, the first and most important phase of his compromise came on the plane of practice; theory inspired by disinterested curiosity was the exception rather than the rule.

To satisfy the craving of hunger, man had to capture the beast of the field and forest, the fowl of the air, and the fish of the sea, and, to do this effectively, fitting tools were fashioned from crude materials. Thus he learned how to make and use the stone axe, as well as the bow and arrow, the spear, the harpoon, and the bolas.[1] Here we must repeatedly remind ourselves that the fashioning and manipulation of such weapons as the bow and arrow, while we tend to pass over them in a matter-of-fact manner, represent a supreme accomplishment for the mind of early man. He also stood in need of a shelter against the cold, the rain and storms of a changing climate, a need he

---

1. J. de Morgan (*Prehistoric Man: A General Outline of Prehistory,* New York, 1925, pp. 35ff.) gives a comprehensive history of the implements and materials used by early man. It is possible that the bow and arrow were used in the Old Stone Age. J. Gillin: *The Ways of Men,* New York, 1948, p. 376; also J. R. Conrad: *The Horn and the Sword,* New York, 1957, p. 15.

supplied first by robbing the beast of his mountain cave, and later by constructing a dwelling with his hands. To clothe his body he plundered the animal of his hide, at least until he learned the arts of spinning and weaving. He soon realized too that another man can be a more deadly enemy than the beast or exposure, and to protect himself against his rivals he devised weapons of war.[2] From the family, whose moral conventions were developed at an early period, arose a more extended group or band which varied in size depending on the type of subsistence activity the members engaged in; such a group in turn could be organized into an effective unit for offensive or defensive warfare. All this, however, was not achieved in one or fifty generations; it involved long ages of organic development, a long span of experiment by trial and error, sad disappointments, and frequent, breathtaking shocks and surprises.

It is hard for us to visualize the conditions prevailing in primitive society. Man moved about over a tiny segment of the earth, beyond which stretched an immeasurable unknown; in fact, the unknown invaded the known on every side, more obviously than at any other time in history, and because it was unknown it was frightening. Today this fear of the unknown, after the tools of civilization have given us more confidence, survives only in ghost stories, religious phobias, nightmares and asylums, while, for early man, the danger from hostile forces was omnipresent. He had no radio or telephone connections with his fellow man; hence every stranger, because his customs were different, was a prospective enemy trespassing on his domain. There was no library to consult, no geologist or astronomer to explain the phenomena of earth and sky. And so when he gazed into the starry heavens or waited for the first sign of spring, he referred to an imagination inspired by fear instead of consulting what we should call the common-sense experience of every man. He was a highly developed animal

---

2. When man's life was so dependent on meeting immediate needs, where sharp distinctions can be traced between the mores of clans and tribes, there is no reason to believe man's earliest state was a peaceful one; any such conclusion must be branded as wishful thinking.

imprisoned within transparent walls. Some degree of freedom
was possible only after successive conquests over nature, his
fellow man, and himself.

And so with all man's practical conquests, life in the stone
ages was far from being a simple matter. Despite a certain
measure of practical security in his immediate circle, he was
threatened on all sides by possible disease, storms, earthquakes,
strange appearances in the sky—all of which he was unable to
cope with or account for. Adverse weather conditions either
flooded or parched the land, tore up trees by the roots and froze
over the waters in winter; thunder and lightning hurled a glower-
ing menace from the wrathful heavens; the earthquake shook
the foundations beneath his feet, while the volcano vomited
forth its fiery spleen over the fruit of his labors. Disease,
attacking from within, left the body a lifeless corpse, the
survivors in an awesome stupor. Death itself, stalking about so
mysteriously and inevitably through the ranks of men, created
a huge question mark in the mind long before the mystery of
questions inspired the poets. Fear, then, was the predominant
emotion of man toward his surroundings, and as long as such
an emotion prevailed, magic and religion were summoned to
reconcile him with a frightful world, as reason and thought were
later destined to serve his curiosity in a parallel capacity.

As the artist strives for self-identification through his medium,
the primitive projected images of his known world against a
background of unknown mystery to deal with the latter more
effectively. Man has always been selfish enough by nature to
wish to control his environment and at the same time to give
himself a better sense of security in a world of change, and in
a world predominated by fear he was far from able to accept
the limitations of experience as basic facts. The sun, the moon,
the trees of the forest, the mountain cave, the ocean and the
river, the animal he ate for food—all became the dwelling-places
of spirits: some kindly, some hostile to his welfare, depending
on whether they benefited or harmed him, and this interpretation was so much more important than mere limitations in time
and space. Such a spirit brought good or bad weather, victory

or defeat in battle, fertility of the womb and the soil, even life and death. Disease, which apparently worked from within outward, was an evil demon taking up a temporary residence in the body, which must be coaxed or forced out to bring relief to the patient. To further the cause of beneficent nature and her guardian spirits, ceremonies of imitation were devised; by such a procedure the community was in a measure assured of the change from winter to spring, the fertility of the soil and the female, the fall of rain, and the preservation of life. In compliance with rigid, arbitrary laws of cause and effect, the forces of destruction were evaded or appeased by a variety of tabus as demanding as the uncompromising dogma of the orthodox churchman.

Furthermore, there was that problem of the alter ego we call the soul. It was quite natural to conclude that if the plant and animal were endowed with a power granting life and motion, man also possessed such an invisible center of power. Whether it took the form of man himself, a winged creature, or a spectral image, it was thought to be somewhat elusive and, in view of the threat of death, a highly prized possession. In times of illness great precautions were taken lest the soul should escape and leave the body lifeless. Once a man was dead, the soul continued to survive, perhaps in a tree or an animal (whence arose the notion of the totem); in some cases it hovered near the grave, or, if not properly cared for, visited near relatives with misfortune. The soul, then, both as subject and object, was a matter of grave concern to the primitive savage; hence the importance of burial rites and sacrifices at the tomb. When a king died in Moravia, all his favorites, including humans and animals, were driven into a cave and slaughtered by the priests around the bier of the deceased. In life it was of paramount importance to keep body and soul together and, once the latter had taken leave of its mortal remains, to insure some measure of happiness for the soul in the next world; in this way survivors could feel safe from its possible return to work them harm.

Here we are confronted not only with the concept of animism but also with the idea of immortality. It seems that as soon as the horror of death impinged itself on human consciousness, the notion of survival was reflected in burial rites, in festivals celebrating the return of spring and in pictures of after-life. How did man convince himself of the fact of immortality? Beyond certain analogies we have suggested from other phenomena, he was never able to prove it in terms of experience, a statement which also holds good for civilized man. Nevertheless an awareness of the infinite and eternal has always been projected by the civilized mind beyond the temporal and finite.[3] For such a mind the infinite and eternal appear to be hovering somewhere on the outer edges of experience, but for primitive man life was so permeated with such realities he could never have realized them as integrated objective facts; hence it was unnecessary to convince or prove to himself their existence. Moreover, the use of magic implies a low respect for the restrictions of time and space. Limitations in experience had presented themselves as problems the primitive had dealt with to suit his practical convenience, but they had never stamped an indelible impression on his mind; hence we find what appears to us a jumble of conflicting thoughts inspired by vivid, intense emotions, showing little relation to one another or to the facts of experience.

The primitive knew it was necessary and pleasant to eat and drink to a certain measure at certain times; beyond this point excess brought with it vengeance, but this common-sense thinking he ignored when he traced disease to an evil demon in possession of the body. He knew he had never seen the body leap out into the infinite and eternal, yet in his viewpoint it was comparatively easy to hurdle physical boundaries. The world of the spirit was so closely affiliated with everyday experience that the souls of the departed lived on in communion with the world of the flesh. There was no fixed borderline between the natural and supernatural in the primitive mind. And since

---

3. This subject has been dealt with in the Introduction.

man's attitude toward the spiritual was permeated with fear, he sought an effective means of controlling it; the coward, once at the helm of control, becomes an uncompromising tyrant. Let us see what manner of weapon was forged to deal directly with the spirit and indirectly with circumstances under spiritual control.

Human desire among primitives was so strong and self-centered that man was easily persuaded of his ability to reach beyond limitations and to control the supernatural by means of magic. How it all began no one can tell, for its inception antedates any record we possess. Perhaps a fortuitous connection between cause and effect in man's efforts, culminating in a desired result, was so convincing that early man, like the modern gambler, was so intoxicated with his own power that he was thenceforth ready to stake everything, over and over again, on this one connection and close his eyes to any possible exceptions. Every performance inspired by magic had for its goal a practical achievement, including a safe conduct to the next world. Magic, by means of words, names, symbols, numbers, movements employed in rituals, and incantations brought about desired changes in weather, fortune and health. It brought rain to the parched ground; it moved the game of the hunter; it improved one's circumstances or ruined others'; it drove out the demons of illness from the diseased body; it compelled the greatest spirits to bend to its sway—both in this world and the next. Eventually one man was chosen, one who, endowed with "power" in the primitive sense of the term, became a master of formula and rite, perhaps because he had been most successful in choosing the best time and place for the best results. The magician, then, came to be a most influential man in primitive tribes, in many cases more powerful than the king himself, if he was not already magician and king at one and the same time. His position was also a precarious one, for once his people lost faith in his "power," his fall could be both sudden and disastrous.

To the modern it seems absurd that a tribe of people should

be enslaved to magic formulae over periods of centuries in the face of so many demonstrations of ineffectiveness.[4] The magician, it must be remembered, was necessarily a man of exceptional ability and a clever psychologist in his way, who realized he might make a mistake or lose his power over the spirit world. The formula, however, or the theory behind the formula was never wrong, for once it had succeeded, the primitive believed it was the only path to success. Like an artist who paints a scene vividly and colorfully without noticing his defects in foreshortening and perspective, the primitive saw his desire realized over and beyond the exception that had no part in making the rule. This desire can exercise a despotic authority over human affairs. After all, the primitive was solving his problems no differently from certain civilized men who deify and bolster their prejudices on a rational plane. Another feature of his viewpoint plays a role here: the thinking that lay behind magical theory was inspired by the subjective ability of the microcosm (man, in this case) to control the macrocosm, or the world at large, each one related to the other like concentric circles, a view which encouraged the application of rigid laws of cause and effect operating back and forth; it substituted the frequent use of analogy for later reasoning and so spurred on the use of imitative "power."

If magic was powerful enough to control the will of a god, of what did the religion of the primitive consist? Frazer[5] draws an interesting distinction between religion and magic by claiming for the former the propitiation of a personal divinity, while to the other he assigns the control of a more or less impersonal power. If we accept such an arbitrary distinction, where does

---

4. R. Allier, (*The Mind of the Savage*, New York, 1929, p. 211) feels certain the primitive would remain in this state unless help were brought in from the outside to change him. If this is true, how did civilized man succeed in reaching his present level? Another theory developed later in the book, that the present-day primitive is a product of degeneration cannot be defended and therefore offers no solution to the problem.

5. Sir James Frazer, *The Golden Bough* (abridged), New York, 1934, pp. 222ff.

one leave off and the other begin? We may assume that magic came first in point of time, but it is hardly likely that the primitive was ever conscious of such a division. Even in later times, when a personal god comes into the picture, it is difficult to know whether the worshipper is humbly requesting or politely demanding a blessing from his divinity. To worship a god in Frazer's sense implies a divinity who takes a personal interest in each of his subjects, who can maintain a relation of mutual trust between himself and man, whereas the primitive first feared the spirit, then fettered him in chains of magic and finally dictated to him. He knew that if his world was to be a safe dwelling-place, he had to be on his guard against evil spirits; if he relaxed his vigilance, some malignant power, the soul of a departed relative or the magic of an enemy, was ready to devour him.

Throughout the history of man's thought, he has sought for some device, magical, religious or otherwise, to serve as a fixed bulwark against the uncertainty of circumstances which breeds fear in the heart. There are indications that, on more advanced levels, the regularity of certain numbers fascinated the primitive, but they were evidently too abstract to have much weight in practice. Because magic operated according to definite rules and apparently produced practical results he could see with his own eyes, he clung to it in preference to the waywardness, the uncertainty, of more scientific experiments. In this connection, we must remind ourselves again and again that modern man still carries along in his rational processes many vestiges of magical thinking.

The notion that nature moves along in her course according to well-regulated laws was no doubt encouraged by the constant recurrence of the seasons. Still there was enough uncertainty in natural phenomena, all of which threatened him with disaster, to inspire the primitive with fear lest spring might not rescue him from the deathlike slumber of winter. Unexpected phenomena like the eclipse of the sun or the fall of meteors occasioned great alarm; in the case of the former, the savage shot arrows into the air to drive away the black monster seeking to devour his benefactor. Likewise, it was squarely up to him, especially in neolithic times, to hasten the return of spring with all the practical benefits it brought in its wake. In some communities the king was regarded as a being powerful enough to keep the laws of nature running in their customary channels. This king was hedged about with a multitude of tabus and, should he show signs of weakness and lose his control, he was forthwith put to death. Certainly the head was uneasy that wore such a crown. Moreover, since winter had to die before spring could be reborn and the microcosm had to move in a circle concentric with the macrocosm, he sacrificed men to please the spirits and feasted on the flesh—all to insure fertility of the soil in the spring. So many of the spring and harvest festivals which have survived as gay holidays in our civilized world are heirlooms of a time when festivity was a synonym for savage cruelty exacted by the relentless forces of nature; man also had to do what he supposed the spirits delighted in doing to insure a modicum of practical security.

Discovery among primitives was a very slow process. The first notable advance on the part of man after descending from the tree came from the use of the hand, set free for more constructive purposes by the assumption of the upright position and bipedal locomotion. He learned how to fashion crude instruments, which, combined with his cunning, enabled him to outwit a rival, regardless of his size or strength. Then came the flash of fire he had long seen in lightning, in forest fires and whenever sparks flashed from the contact of two stones; he probably learned how to generate a flame by striking two pieces of flint together.[6] The use of fire in the family group initiated the sacred history of the hearth, the gathering place of the family; fire also prepared his food and frightened away the prowling beast at night. Eventually came the use of the tongue against the teeth and the roof of the mouth to utter articulate

---

6. C. S. Coon (*The Story of Man,* New York, 1954, pp. 61–62) claims there is no evidence that man of the early and middle Pleistocene was able to make a fire. Cf. C. R. Knight: *Prehistoric Man,* New York 1948, p. 103.

sounds.[7] The first words, if we may call them such, must have included all the meaning we can pack into a simple or even a complex sentence, suggesting a panoramic picture flashed upon a sensitive aural screen. The use of the hand raised man above the level of the animal and made of him a practical technician. Fire and speech, in addition to other advantages, made him a social being on the threshold of early civilization.[8]

With the advent of the new stone age we find man availing himself of sand to polish his stone weapons. Society was organized into tribes, over which presided a king or chief, or clans, a unit claiming the highest loyalty of the individual. As a rule, he practiced exogamy, a custom of marrying outside the family or clan, which was a partial guarantee of security in succession but not designed to avoid any weakness supposedly resulting from inbreeding.[9] The nomad had a tendency to settle down either around lakes to support himself by fishing and herding, or on fertile soil, where he eventually turned to agriculture. Certain animals, especially the dog, were domesticated and drawn into the service of their master. From clay, man learned to fashion pots of various shapes; from reeds growing around the swamps, he wove his baskets with certain designs later imitated on pottery; he also set up megaliths and other monuments as a tribute to unknown divinities. Because no written records have survived, we know nothing of his moments of reflection; beyond his reliance on magic, we can only half guess at how he solved his first problems, his attitude toward wife and children, his fellow man, his divinity or how he met the challenge of the unexpected. His grave is our best source of information: his bones tell us something of his anatomy and appearance; his tools speak of his daily activities; the food and

---

7. W. Howells (*Back of History*, New York, 1954, pp. 56–68) gives an excellent discussion of language.

8. C. S. Coon (*op. cit.*, p. 15) also adds "sharp-focusing eyes."

9. The fear of incest is called by G. A. Richard (F. Boas *et al: General Anthropology*, New York, 1938, p. 448) a matter of respect. For J. Layard (E. E. Evans-Pritchard *et al: The Institutions of Primitive Society*, Glencoe, 1954, pp. 52–53) incest is a threat to the social stability of the tribe.

drink suggest his belief in immortality in the form of individual survival and how closely the material and spiritual realms were intertwined; and his art, if we can speak of it in our sense of the term, gives us some indication of how he spent his time at home.

Art among civilized peoples is a form of self-identification in a medium which will best reflect man's ambitions and viewpoint as a whole. It is another expression of the compromise effected between human desire and the world it seeks to mold in its own image. But among primitives it is more directly subservient to their desires and serves a more practical purpose; in other words, its origin was probably dictated by magic. On the surface, if we may judge from the standpoint of technique, we may think the primitive has come close to our standards of pictorial art; for some time the cave paintings of Altamira were put down as modern forgeries. Let us take a glance at paleolithic work before we treat its more distinctive character. The earliest creations we have are sculptured human figures, the best preserved, in Vienna, being a nude female with downcast face, prominent breasts and abdomen, and thick thighs, possibly a survival of sex or fertility worship. The modeling of the whole figure and the treatment of the hair are surprisingly well done for the period. Strange to say, the human figure is antecedent to the animal in representation. On a rock in southern France we find animals, especially horses, worked out in high relief. Later the artist combined low relief with incised lines in the same field of representation. Painting also occupied his attention, first by applying broad patches of color without toning and gradually working up to a polychrome stage. Most of the animals, such as the horse, the bison, the reindeer, are depicted in action by men who had faced these creatures in the hunt and had acquired a vivid picture of their movements and then painted from memory. It was a perceptual art, like that of the Bushmen and the Minoans.

After passing in review a number of these paintings, we notice certain features which suggest the artist was not interested merely in decorating the walls of his cave. Usually those animals

he hunted for food were chosen for his scenes; the lion, which
figured so strongly in Assyrian reliefs, was overlooked in favor
of the horse, the bison, the deer, and occasionally the wolf and
mammoth. In some cases the arrow, the implement of the
hunter, was painted on the beast of prey. Most of these repre-
sentations were found in the dark recesses of caves, where
artificial light is necessary to see them and torches were required to paint them. With all his skill in handling line and
color, the artist is not proficient in building up a composition
in his groupings, and frequently one animal or a group of animals is painted over another. Furthermore, when carving a
horse's head on horn, the teeth both in front and back are
clearly visible, the model being the head after the removal of
the hide. The drawing of plants, which intrigued such people as
the Minoans, was neglected, and where they are depicted, it
is well nigh impossible to identify them.[10] Obviously the cave
was the earliest hall of ceremonies we know of, where incantations were recited and rites performed—all for a very practical
purpose. Magic, the servant of subjective desire, suggested
that by painting animals on a wall they would be as much in
man's power as a god of Egypt was, once his secret name was
revealed to the pharaoh. By making art the tool of magic the
primitive was assured of a rich game supply for future hunting.[11]

One well-executed but damaged scene, incised on horn, is
indicative of the artist's purpose: three stags are moving along,
one behind the other, in a field which contains no landscape
detail, unless we interpret the fish swimming between their
legs as symbols of water. The stag in the rear is looking around
him as if apprehensive of danger from a distant quarter and
perhaps sounding an alarm to the rest of the herd. The artist
was not at all hesitant about foreshortening the head of the
animal against the left shoulder. The symbol behind the antlers
may stand for the bow and arrow (perhaps a dart but surely
not a signature). But why the fish between the legs? One might
conjecture the magician-artist was interested in a supply of fish

---

10. J. de Morgan: *op. cit.*, p. 200.
11. Another view is held by C. R. Knight: *op. cit.*, p. 168.

as well as big game, but certainly he cared little for water as
a setting for his subject. Scott's lines, I believe, will furnish us
with a satisfactory clue.

> The stag at eve had drunk his fill,
> Where danced the moon on Monon's rill.

The artist was no doubt an experienced hunter accustomed to
see his kill standing knee-deep in the waters of a pool, whither
they frequently repaired at the close of day, and in this scene
he presented them as being surprised at their favorite rendezvous. His wishful thinking, carved in concrete material, would
charm one unwitting stag after another to his doom at the
water's edge.

The fact that magic was the motivating power behind so
much of his art need not detract from its aesthetic value. It is
interesting, when studying the development of flints, to observe
how mere usefulness is accompanied by beauty of form, how
shells and the teeth and vertebrae of animals were adapted
to personal adornment. We can only marvel at the artist's skill
in bringing out the salient features of appearance with the
strictest economy of line, his sense for fitting a single figure into
a given space, his way of repeating certain features, like antlers,
to render an impressionistic effect. There was no halting consciousness to pose a hesitating question somewhere between
the vivid image of memory and the hand of execution. In the
use of color also he was a seasoned worker, applying it to an
animal both to lend it the illusion of modeling and, due to its
varying intensities, to give his subject a polychrome effect. On
the plane of naturalism he knew what to concentrate on for
emphasis and what to omit to produce a charming, impressive
representation—like the later Greek sculptor of the fifth century
working on the plane of the ideal.

The ability of the artist, far from maintaining such a high
level of drawing, degenerated periodically to the use of abbreviated forms, possibly due to repeated copying. During the neolithic period, sometimes considered a more decadent stage in
art, this level of art persists from one generation to another,

although we must admit the range of subjects is much broader. These men worked on pottery made by hand from stone and later from fired clay (the wheel was a much later invention). There are also signs of decorative patterns employed for their own sake, which means that art had taken one step to divorce itself from magic. The dwellings of these people, patterned after the tent, were set into the ground and covered with a cone-shaped roof, a hole being left in the top to allow the smoke to escape. The lake-dwellers built their simple homes on extensive platforms supported by piles.[12] They buried their dead in artificial grottoes, sometimes covering the entire body with the objects laid beside it, at other times scraping the flesh from the bones before burial.

Neolithic man, although still a hunter at times, gained most of his livelihood either as a herdsman or a farmer, a more settled mode of life than that of the hunter, which means he was much busier than his predecessor of the cave. Work required more of his time, but the dangers of existence had lessened. His new means of gaining a living also encouraged a division of labor theretofore unknown. He had to sow, till, and reap his crops, build a home and keep it in repair, care for domestic animals, fashion more tools, etc., but all this does not account for the decline of his art. Magic still held a strong grip on the mind, but now it was no longer directed chiefly to the animal, some of which were domesticated, as the major source of food. The animal is something concrete enough to observe and retain as an image in the artist's memory; when the emphasis changed from the beast of prey to the soil, man directed his magic to the change of seasons and the fertility of the earth. How could he represent the annual return of spring which he could not visualize or objectify in any tangible form of art? No doubt, he staked all his hopes on ritual and incantation until the concept of the great mother and the heroic myth were eventually cast in human form. The change of seasons is

---

12. C. S. Coon (*op. cit.,* p. 118) illustrates a further development of the Neolithic house.

a sequence of events in time which lends itself more to narrative expression, if we may call upon Lessing for support, than to representation in the plastic arts, a fact which tends to date the origin of the world's greatest myths to this period in man's history.

We have found, in dealing with primitive man, that art can hardly stand alone as a vehicle for aesthetic expression any more than magic can be separated from religion. There is no valid reason, as some authorities assume, why a high development in art techniques should preclude the dominance of magical influence. It is only on the conscious level of limitations in experience that one can learn to compare, differentiate, and classify mental functions we tend to take for granted in our long inheritance and are prone to project as perfected functions into the mental equipment of the savage. Experience in such terms was to him a flimsy covering behind which his magic, art, and religion were brought to a single focus to serve a practical purpose. We are fascinated by the mysterious question marks behind the mask of death; the primitive, who was as intimate with this mysterious unknown as W. H. Hudson with the pulse of nature, sensed a real world behind it. Likewise, it is dangerous to use the analogy of the child when probing into the mystery of origins, because the child of today grows up amid the inheritance of centuries; he imitates so much that has been learned since the beginning of man's history, while primitive man could draw only upon a limited storehouse of tradition; and the child of today, in spite of such an apparent advantage, could never face practical problems with the same courage as the primitive.[13] It was a long and tedious process, to be sure, whose lasting value can no more be appreciated at our level of civilization than a college graduate can fairly estimate his first grammar school efforts in prose composition.

Before we examine the personality of the primitive more closely, we must recall that his world was much more compact

---

13. F. Boas: *The Mind of Primitive Man*, New York, 1911, p. 175; O. Klineberg: *Race Differences*, New York, 1935, pp. 332ff.

than our own; in other words, the eternal and the infinite were more closely identified with the temporal and finite. We think we know something about the limitations of time and space; the former, we say, extends back to a point where geology leaves no record and into the future as far as the imagination will lead us; finite space takes us out to the most distant star visible through a telescope and to the most minute particles revealed by the microscope. Beyond these limitations stretches the fathomless, the incalculable—for some it is God. Among primitives, the horizon of time and space was but little removed from the scene of his daily activities, and the sun, instead of being millions of miles from the earth, was within the reach of an arrow. For us, God, although he can make himself manifest in finite terms, dwells in a heaven far beyond the home of man; the world of the primitive was saturated with divinity. For these reasons the forms of his experience assume such a superficial character on the periphery of spiritual power where the operations of the spirit, the most real aspect of life, could only be interpreted and controlled by the tools of magic. With this in mind, let us probe further into the primitive mentality to see how he built up relationships between human nature with its desires and the world at large.

The mind of the primitive, far from being opposite to our own in its operations, was an early and more simple stage of our own mental development, very much under the dominant control of personal emotions and convictions. It is useless to say he was not realistic, for no man's world was more real than that of the savage; likewise, it is futile to say there was no cause-and-effect relationship, no purpose in his thoughts and actions. All this was more simple, but more rigid and orthodox than among us. He made use of all these adjuncts and more—to a different degree—in his planning, and what is more, he focused all his efforts in thought directly upon action. The primitive was essentially a pragmatic man whose motivations operated along a few direct and well-worn channels. One important difference, then, between the thinking of the primitive (and many early civilized peoples) and the modern is revealed in an increased emphasis on the theoretical among modern man, a development for which the Greek was primarily responsible.

When the modern, faced with an unexplained turn of events, tries to establish a cause-and-effect relationship, he takes for granted the possibility of a number of causes as factors producing a certain situation within the field of his attention, and the same is true when he makes an estimate of possible effects to be brought about by a given cause or causes; for this reason he patiently weighs various possibilities in terms of thought and experiment in his laboratory. For the primitive, the number of causes and effects applicable to a given situation were usually, though not necessarily, narrowed down to two or three; once he became aware of a certain effect, such as an injury inflicted by an enemy or an eclipse of the sun, a possible cause could be more easily and directly traced, and a definite line of connection between the two could be established for future reference. When the objective is under the sway of the insistent subjective, complexity and uncertainty tend to give way to the simple and dependable. The primitive projected a personal, monistic interpretation upon the objective world which, as we believe, is actually pluralistic and full of possibilities of greater or lesser significance. His intent was whole and consistent in all its parts and therefore admitted no exception when brought to bear on the objective which, to the primitive, was of little importance for its own sake. His mind was neither pre-logical, as Levy-Bruhl would have it, nor illogical; it used logic in an elementary stage of development, governed by the certainty of personal, subjective desire.

There was a certain immediacy about the connection established between the objective phenomenon and the subjective reaction, reinforced by emotional pressure behind it, so that there was seldom any doubt in the primitive's mind about the truth either of the connection or the impression received. Franz Boas[14] asserts that "in primitive culture the impressions of the outer world are associated intimately with subjective impres-

---

14. *op. cit.*, p. 238.

sions, which they call forth regularly. . . ." Consequently, the connection between subject and object can easily be resolved into an identity, or what Jung calls "unconscious equality," [15] which, if unpleasant, may be equivalent to being possessed by the devil, but, if pleasant, may become a mystic union much like the relationship existing between a mother and her child or between the seer and the seen.[16] If a kindred spirit was sensed in some animal or bird, it could easily become the totem, first of the individual and then of the whole tribe. When the native of Central America identified himself with the quetzal bird, he was not expressing a strong preference for this creature; the two—subject and object—were one and the same, for emotional identification in the mind of the primitive was much more complete than that of his civilized descendant, whether the object was viewed as a natural phenomenon or as a symbol.

The nature of the totem and man's interpretation of its wishes dictated certain activities to be carried out and others to be avoided, until a body of tradition was accumulated that made a particular tribe distinct from all others. Once a custom had been firmly established, though its origin was forgotten in time, it was dangerous, sometimes fatal, to violate it. The primitive has always clung to conservatism as a means of protection in the face of a changing world and the possible displeasure of otherwise beneficent spirits. "Any society that feels itself in danger instinctively tends to enforce conformity in thought and conduct upon its members, and to suppress all thought and conduct that might disturb the internal harmony of the group." [17] The tendency of the modern to regard with disapproval the man who fails to conform to standards in clothing is a survival of this attitude. The stranger bringing new customs was dangerous to the primitive; he might be set upon and put to death, because the newcomer posed a threat to the control

---

15. Cf. C. R. Aldrich: *The Primitive Mind and Modern Civilization,* New York, 1931, p. 79.

16. Cf. M. Buber: *I and Thou* (trans. by R. G. Smith), Edinburgh, 1952, p. 18.

17. C. R. Aldrich: *op. cit.,* p. 97.

a particular group had achieved over the macrocosm. The close identification of the individual with the group militated against the development of individualism, which in turn discouraged the accumulation of wealth by a single person; property was owned on a collective basis, hence theft was not as criminal an offense as among our peoples.[18]

We know that man is an organism born to cope with adverse circumstances and make his living until the energy of life fades into death. We know that animals are organisms capable of motion but not endowed with the higher powers of thought. We see plants and trees that also live and die on a fixed location. In addition, we are aware of a host of inorganic objects devoid of life, comparatively stationary and subject only to the laws of gravity. For our distant ancestor there was no distinction between organic and inorganic; every object in nature had *mana* to a greater or lesser degree; everything, including himself, had its visible and invisible manifestations, the latter being the more important.

Man's conclusions about certain phenomena in experience proceeded largely from the manifestations of his own ego. When he fell asleep, he was conscious of another self in his dreams, engaging in various activities and moving from the spot where his sleeping body was lying; he also saw other men in his dreams, men who, according to their statements the following morning, had been asleep all night. He naturally concluded that this alter ego or soul had escaped from the body in the night when vigilance was relaxed. What is more, it must be a more powerful part of his make-up than the body itself, which was unable to move without the soul. But how did the soul escape the body? Obviously through certain openings like the nose and mouth. Hence, as we have already said, in times of

---

18. Cf. R. Turner: *The Great Cultural Traditions,* New York, 1941, Vol. I, p. 75. There is another reason for the lack of emphasis on individual accumulation of wealth: if he had a great number of valuable possessions over and above that of the average man, what could he do with them except display them on his person or increase his prestige by generosity? Cf. also Klineberg: *op. cit.,* p. 269.

sickness precautions were taken to waylay the soul in its attempt to escape from its material home. The soul came to be regarded as capable of survival after it left the body a lifeless heap of flesh and bones, which accounts for the concern of man for departed souls, for ritual cults associated with the tomb, and his constant fear of losing his own soul.

Spirits were responsible for much of the strange behavior the primitive saw in himself and others. He noticed some men, in a conscious state, giving way to ecstasy, to paroxysms of fears, to rash courage, and he saw that some of their acts, under such influences, were good, while others were detrimental. He was no doubt familiar with visions of ghosts lingering near the tomb, with hallucinations and mirages, all due to the machinations of the spirit world. Since spirits were both good and evil, it was up to him to curry their favor and avoid their displeasure. When a pregnant woman dies in contemporary Samoa, the foetus, which may become a disagreeable ghost, must be cut from the dead body before burial of the mother.[19] Moreover, the spirit was dynamic in its operations; when it conceived a desire within its province to fulfill, the desire went into effect spontaneously without resorting to a mechanical, piece by piece procedure or meditation between conception and realization. The spirit was always on the *qui vive,* while man had to spend certain hours in sleep and so became more vulnerable to the designs of a hostile agent. Its ways were highly mysterious, but the cause and effect connection could be imitated by anyone seeking control over the particular spirit. Similar causes, the primitive thought, must always bring about similar effects, both operating between the microcosm and the macrocosm.

The immediacy of the impact of an impression on the mind of the primitive made one particular impression paramount to his attention and shut out the possibility (for the time, at least) of another equally cogent truth or value coming from another direction; comparative values and time and space limitations played a subordinate role. The same immediacy we have found

19. M. Mead: *Coming of Age in Samoa,* New York, 1928, p. 133.

in his art perceptions, in his ability to achieve self-identification
with an animal or any object that afforded him satisfaction.
Again the ordinary barriers of concrete experience were of little
consequence. He sensed the same directness between his planned
action (especially in magic) and its results in the objective
sphere, so that when a single cause, issuing from the subject,
brought forth an effect he construed as successful and agreeable, he identified himself completely with this line of procedure, he standardized it until it became a sacred tradition
to the neglect of any other possible connection between other
possible causes and effects. Man's desire for success had been
so impressed by this one cause-and-effect sequence that he was
willing to make great sacrifices to help the subject maintain
control of the object along this well-worn pathway between
the microcosm and the macrocosm.

One might easily conclude that because material manifestations were negligible, primitive man, at an early stage, was on
the road to abstract thinking. On the contrary, he continued
to concentrate on the same practical ends; consequently, the
approved connections between a given cause and effect became
so sacredly traditional that any experimental tampering with
theoretical means was out of the question. Even our contemporary primitive is amazed when the scientist or explorer
presumes he is wrapped in meditation. Moreover, his language,
since attributes could be considered as objects separate from
their nouns, gave little quarter to the development of abstract
thought; the use of numbers in counting was also comparatively
superfluous when he knew the traits and attributes of the objects
in his experience.[20] If the magician wished to control the activities of the spirit, he had to use concrete objects to imitate those
particular spiritual movements which were beneficial to man's
practical welfare in an approved pattern of cause and effect.

---

20. F. Boas *op. cit.*, p. 149: "Primitive man, when conversing with his
fellowman, is not in the habit of discussing abstract ideas. His interests
center around the occupations of his daily life; and where philosophical
problems are touched upon, they appear either in relation to definite individuals or in the more or less anthropomorphic forms of religious beliefs."

Extraordinary privileges and responsibilities were assigned to this man. Some believed that the *mana* of this individual was so powerful that the mere touch of his person or eating the left-overs of his meal would bring death to the victim.

To call this fantasy or abstract thinking is hardly justified, for, after all, the primitive did not attend to an object with the express purpose of gathering food for the imagination or intellect but to make practical use of it. Neither can one deny that he had established a subject-object relationship in his thinking. Such a relationship would be required even in fantasy thinking; on the other hand, since he had little concern for the object *per se,* one would not say an even balance was maintained between subject and object. The fact that magic played such a prominent role in the efficacy of his thought means that the subject, like the absolute ruler who has good reason to fear his people, set up a tyranny of expediency over the object; we should be very reluctant to call the primitive either a scientific or speculative thinker.[21] One important reason for his slow development through the ages was his supreme confidence in magic to control the object. In a sense, he lived in a house of mirrors where he saw the reflections of his own gratified wants. Of course, he was not always able to gain his ends in practice, but he never lost faith in the efficacy of using an object, human or otherwise as a means to a practical end. Had he been more critical of the means, he would have learned to see the object in a clearer perspective and to experiment more with theory.

It seems, then, that the primitive created spiritual powers to account for the transiency and caprice of the objective world and then, to allay his fear of their designs, invented means for subduing these same spirits to his own will. A stupid way of deceiving oneself, says the modern, who puts his trust in an omnipotent, perfect divinity; yet this same modern, in his prayers, unconsciously reduces this same divinity to vest-pocket size. The whole process represents an inner conflict in the

---

21. P. Radin (*Primitive Man as Philosopher,* New York, 1957, pp. 275ff.) is willing to call him a philosopher, but he deals with the primitive already in contact with our civilization.

psyche of the primitive: he experienced a fear which he projected into the realm of the objective, whereupon he devised a subjective method for coping with it, a procedure the unscientific modern follows again and again on the rational level; the self-deception is more obvious in primitive practice, because it all happens on the same plane but is less paradoxical than the procedure of the modern, whose second, apologetic self must justify itself in the face of a perfect divinity primitive man never acknowledged. In the meantime, the latter gained self-confidence, or, to put it better, he found his self-confidence reflected in and corrobated by the objective, and that reflection, however disadvantageous in other directions, was an asset for any people whose sense of security would otherwise have been very weak.

After this review we can draw together the various manifestations of the primitive's expression and view his efforts in thought and action in a clearer perspective. We have seen that he was very conservative in his way of doing things; we found him to be very subjective in his viewpoint, fearing the unpredictable motions and changes he saw in the objective and overcoming the object of fear by subjective means. Magic, the tool he himself devised, was applied over and over to uniform laws of cause and effect; his rituals were repeated according to the same formulae year after year. The primitive, whether he realized it or not, was engaged in a constant struggle against capricious change in time and space; a dependable regularity, approaching what we should call a monotonous sameness, spelled security in his living. We may say, to put it in other words, that he lived, as so many subjective people have always lived, closely identified with his own interpretation of infinity and eternity (sameness and regularity) to which he held fast by his magic.

We have also seen that primitive man, like all men, was fundamentally selfish and forever looking for certainty in the field of knowledge which he could use in practice. He sought for some kind of self-identification with his certainty and security which, because they were opposed to the uncertainty and change of finite experience, we can call, for want of better terms, the changelessness of the eternal and infinite. The paradox of the finite and infinite has created the major problems of man throughout his history, and each culture has effected a compromise between the two in a different way. Before going any further, let us see how we can present the infinite by way of contrast with the finite for the sake of clarity.

I know of no more simple presentation of this subject than that of Parmenides who describes "being" much as we commonly picture the infinite.[22] He refers to it in terms of negatives: it has no beginning, no end in time; hence one cannot speak of it as past, present, or future. It cannot move so that one part of it cannot change places with another; in fact, one cannot speak of its parts for that very reason, for it is infinite, which means it fills up all conceivable emptiness; motion and change of place would be contradictory to its nature. If it is not created from anything else, it remains the same, eternal, immutable, self-identical. It cannot be divided, for there is no room for an agent of division outside infinity. It never grows less; it never increases; it remains everywhere, eternally itself. It has no positive attributes, because such an attribute would imply the possibility of difference—it simply is. The finite, on the other hand, is the very opposite to such "being" in every respect.

And what has all this to do with the viewpoint of man? The fact that, throughout his history, he has been involved in this paradox, although unconsciously before the days of the Greek, has made his life problematic, but at the same time interesting. There is in each one of us a desire to live in a world that is somewhat dependable, more dependable than what we find in changing circumstances, and this desire expresses itself in our thoughts and actions; if we can achieve a relative permanence and regularity, we feel more comfortable and secure. This desire has always been natural to man as a subject, and wherever we turn in the history of cultures we can distinguish

---

22. I refer the reader to W. T. Stace: *A Critical History of Greek Philosophy*, London, 1924, pp. 44-45.

between the orderly arrangement of his creations and the more haphazard growth of nature around them. It would be ridiculous to call man a creature of the infinite, but the subjective self has something in common with that infinite and therefore finds the change of finite imperfections a constant challenge. The very fact that we say "I" or use a personal name implies that we think of ourselves as anchors, however relative the permanence, in a sea of shifting waters. We should all like to know what we were in a possible prior existence or exactly what will happen to human life in a possible next world, but in spite of our ignorance on this score we intend to go on keeping ourselves intact as individuals and resisting dissolution up to the very end. The primitive also resisted change with all his powers, and whatever we may think of his success, he achieved more security (at a higher price) than we have today.

Because the objective was so near and its changing character so immediate, the daily experience of the primitive was saturated with the eternal and infinite.[23] Let us see how he strove in another direction to convert unpredictable change into something more like the sameness of the infinite.

Primitive time was not, as it is for us, an abstract unit of measure. We divide the year into months, the month into days, the day into hours, minutes, and seconds; we can think of these units of measure apart from the subject that is measuring or the thing that is being measured, *i.e.*, we do not have to think of a clock to deal mentally with the units of time. The change from one season to another, from day into night, which were most vital to him, the primitive could not regard as lifeless; they were brought about by spirits succeeding one another in a position which might bring good or ill to every man, spirits which did not die in the same sense as our summer dies but were revived or resurrected and therefore would return again

---

23. Cf. A. H. Compton: "Time and the Growth of Physics" in *Time and Its Mysteries*, New York, 1940, p. 114: "It is noteworthy that the problem of when things began does not seem to concern primitive peoples very much." Cf. also Meyer Fortes in E. E. Evans-Pritchard *et al: op. cit.*, p. 86.

after an uncertain interval. Small wonder that man was so concerned about an eclipse of the sun, which meant a monster was threatening to swallow its spirit and so put an end to the day and year. It was to his advantage not only to bring back the spring after the winter spirit was driven out but also to have it return at a regular time. His subjective mind, since it saw no way of eliminating this kind of motion and change from his experience, sought to make that same motion rigid and standard for the practical benefit of all concerned.

Magic supplied the means and in this case it took the form of a rite supervised by some authorized leader or magician who must have enlisted the assistance of other members of the tribe. The whole procedure, no doubt devised by the magician himself, was an imitation in the form of a prescribed series of motions, accompanied by appropriate words or sounds, of a desired course of events in the macrocosm. What the details of such a rite originally were is lost in the dim, dark past, but the figure of Salmoneus in Greek mythology presents us with just such a primitive magician imitating certain phenomena to bring together the rain clouds.[24] How did early man decide to bring about such results by imitation? Here I am willing to hazard a guess: The shadow of man, which must have caused him some concern by its imitation of all his movements, may have suggested man's ability to coerce the elements into an imitative, obedient compliance.[25] However that may be, these rituals were repeated over and over, century after century, and survived into civilized times, when their origin and much of their significance had been forgotten. Much of this ritual passed into the early material for the theatre.[26]

The words recited along with the ritual were learned by

---

24. Vergil: *Aeneid*, Book VI, 585-594.

25. Cf. H. C. Brearley: *Time Telling Through the Ages*, New York, 1919, p. 16. Primitive man was aware of the shadow's importance for telling time.

26. Lord Raglan: *The Hero*, London, 1936, pp. 225ff. For ceremonies devoted to increase in the production of grain or animals consult G. Thomson: *Aeschylus and Athens*, London, 1946, p. 13.

every member of the tribe and handed down as myths to later generations. The elements concerned were personified; these cosmic personalities were represented as engaging in a struggle whose outcome would be favorable to man's best interests, the outstanding figure assuming the role of a hero or divinity who overpowered the monstrous elemental forces and so ushered in, year after year, the welcome spring. Bernard Schweitzer,[27] after centering the original labors of Herakles around Augeas, classifies the Greek hero with Indra, Siegfried, Rama, Beowulf, and other figures of early epics; he also concludes that these heroes, in their original capacity, free the rays of the sun from the giant of winter and the waters of the streams from the icy hydra.[28] Regardless of what one may think of Schweitzer's thesis, it is quite apparent that a large number of myths go back to man's efforts to regularize the changing movements of the seasons. They reflect not only his desire for security but his emotional reaction of fear in the darkness and desolation of winter and his overwhelming joy at the first sign of spring.

In the thinking of the primitive there is also a strong suggestion of infinity in the subjective character of his decisions, in the certainty with which he looked forward to practical results.[29] The indifferent sceptic whom Dante placed outside the gates of the *Inferno* could not afford to live in such a precarious existence. Man was as sure of his procedures as some divinities, or let us say he was a perfect subject dictating from the pedestal of infinity and eternity to the fickle and dangerous objective; doubt, uncertainty, hesitation, apathy together with humor, which sometime go together, were squelched to enforce a rigid conformity. On numerous occasions the designs of perfect subjectivity might go awry in a finite universe, but that neither diminished the confidence of the subject or cause, nor cast any doubt on the necessary efficacy of a later attempt: good

---

27. *Herakles,* Tuebingen, 1922, p. 238.

28. Ibid., p. 212.

29. J. Dewey: "Time and Individuality" in *Time and Its Mysteries,* New York, 1940, p. 86: "The eternal and immutable is the consummation of mortal man's quest for certainty."

intentions are still good, no matter how often they falter over stumbling blocks.

In summary, the primitive achieved some kind of security in the midst of changing experience, certainty in the midst of the unpredictable by means of magic, a creation of human desire that stressed the importance of the means over the object as an end. It maintained a concentric parallelism between man as the controlling microcosm and the macrocosm beyond; it proclaimed the superiority of the subjective over the objective; it asserted the triumph of the absolute and fixed period over the possibilities of the question mark; it gave man a steady anchor in the infinity, the eternity of changelessness and so served as an antidote for the obsession of fear, but its overemphasis on the subjective prevented the object from speaking for itself and left man unfit for well-balanced, scientific thinking. Such a viewpoint, which held subsequent thought in a vise for centuries, may seem to be diametrically opposed to the scientific outlook on experience only because we see its manifestations much more clearly than its point of departure and then jump to the conclusion that the thinking of the primitive is so basically different from our own it played no part in the historical development of man's mind. When we look at the point of departure, we can see that a mere shift of weight to balance the scale between subject and object, as we shall see later, can produce a much different viewpoint with a new set of comparative values.

It must be stressed, then, that the primitive is not this or that in direct contrast to the modern; the differences must be measured, not in terms of opposites, but of degrees. Potentially, he was everything the modern has become, but his potentialities, like the buds of flowers, had not unfolded into the complex cultural patterns and the specialized intellectual structure of our day. It is hard to say he was not a thinker, although he was not the obvious thinker we find in Rodin's statue nor the systematic thinker pondering abstract significance. One cannot deny he was sensible, even if his reasoning, saturated as it was with magic, reveals a distorted notion of causality and little clear, logical structure, in our sense of the term. One must credit him

with an awareness of the objective, even if the subjective element was so strong it had a ready and prescribed answer for
every problem, all of which gave him the appearance of
unruffled certainty and, after a slight acquaintance with a new
object in experience, an air of unperturbed self-sufficiency. His
conduct, largely governed by the sensations of pain and pleasure,
hardly cherished any respect for a moral code based on abstract
concepts of good and evil. If he was conscious of aesthetic
significance attached to natural phenomena or human action, it
was an irrelevant by-product of attention, of little value for its
own sake. His life, so far as we can see, was too serious to permit
any relaxation by way of humor. That he was an individual we
must admit, but not enough of an individual to stand up in
open defiance of the powers that be or to assert his right to
make his own decisions in the face of tribal tabus. And so, if
he can no longer be called the noble savage in the sense meant
by Tacitus or Voltaire, he is at least a forebear worthy of our
respect and further study.

THE EGYPTIAN

IF ARISTOTLE HAD SEARCHED through his past for an analogy to illustrate the influence of form on matter, he could have found nothing more convincing than the stamp left on Egyptian history by the Nile River. Nowhere on earth has such a waterway, running through the whole length of the land as well as the panorama of its history, become so definitely the artery of a people's civilization. From the earliest days of man's career in this valley, the river has attracted and held people near its banks; it determined the symmetry of the land and the crops to be sown; it has been the chief avenue of transportation from north to south; by its support all manner of men—Egyptians, Assyrians, Persians, Greeks, Christians, and Muslims—have thrived on its banks, raised up their monuments and wasted away among their ruins. It was this river that contributed most to the self-sufficiency of the Egyptian and made his economy primarily agricultural, a feature somewhat different from the life of the Mesopotamian.[1] The Nile was also endowed by the ancients with divinity. So right was its course from south to north that when the Egyptian of the empire stood on the banks of the Euphrates for the first time, he thought of it as a river flowing downhill the wrong way. In the mind of the ancient Egyptian the Nile, its sources buried in mystery and its delta so vast in extent, was a thin thread of eternity steering a straight, changeless course through the vicissitudes of time.

Time and eternity stood out in bold, contrasting relief in the flourishing plenty of plant and animal life on the narrow fringe of land hugging the low banks of the river—against the barren

---

1. R. Turner: *The Great Cultural Traditions,* New York, 1941, Vol. I, p. 181.

cliffs, the sandy desert, and the unwearied course of the sun by day and the stars by night, but the river, ever moving and ever the same, supporting the creatures of time with its life-giving waters, had the advantage in the respect of the nation.[2] There is, then, good reason why the constant urge in all men to make of the ever changing the unchangeable was so much more effective in the Egyptian's efforts. The native looked ahead to life beyond the grave as if this life in time, as pleasant as it may have been, was only a foretaste of things to come, and he made sure it would be abundant with the material pleasures he had learned to enjoy here; there was nothing ascetic about the Egyptian on either side of the grave. He also emphasized the eternal aspects of his destiny by erecting lasting monuments, mostly in the form of tombs, to keep his memory alive in ages to come, but, of course, only the rich and powerful were equal to such an achievement. The diorite figures of the Pharaohs, the gestures and movements of painted men and women, the pyramids and temples suggest a permanence which, in ancient times, was capable of defying the ravages of time, an intimation of something more lasting beyond the gates of death. Human existence was a house of transparent glass, its most pleasant aspects reflected by the mirror of subjective desire into the beyond, and the Egyptian was not one to see through a glass darkly.

The land of Egypt was protected on nearly all sides by natural barriers, making it comparatively secure from invasion and encouraging a self-sufficiency attained by no other civilized people in history. On the north was the sea, which offered no serious threat until the days of empire; on the west was the great desert; on the south was Nubia, a region rich in gold and ivory but of no consequence from a military standpoint; and to the east lay the mountains and the Red Sea. Only from the northeast could an enemy effect an easier penetration, but here too the desert of the Sinai Peninsula presented a serious obstacle. Moreover, since the land itself supplied him with most luxuries and necessities, the Egyptian had no need to go outside his own borders except to obtain wood suitable for construction. These

2. H. Frankfort: *Kingship and the Gods*, Chicago, 1948, p. 117.

facts no doubt fostered a feeling of national unity at an early period, an asset missing in the Sumerian cities, and magnified that attitude of exclusive superiority so dominant among many Oriental peoples. The Egyptian was always certain, even in the period of empire, that his own religion, his art, his institutions, his river Nile, his land and its inhabitants were the best the earth could offer; so much was this taken for granted that comparisons were superfluous.

In paleolithic times, when the land of North Africa produced more abundant vegetation, the plateaus were inhabited by primitive hunters who have left their flint implements for the modern anthropologist to study; nothing of the advanced art of his cave-dwelling brother in Europe has survived.[3] When the Nile eventually settled down into its present channel and life was restricted to a narrow margin along its banks, neolithic man made sufficient strides ahead to make up for any deficiencies of his remote ancestors. Among others, the Badarians, a people of negroid stock, came into the foreground of a more civilized way of life after hunting habits and a more settled pursuit of agriculture had been combined. Their graves, a considerable number of which have been found, reveal a well-developed belief in immortality, a fondness for personal ornament and luxury, and a knowledge of the potter's technique. A native clay furnished the material for some of the finest vases in the history of Egyptian pottery, and this, too, before the wheel was introduced. Malachite, a standard article in Egyptian economy, was brought from the Sinai Peninsula for facial decoration, a sample of which was usually laid beside the dead man's body; the first use of copper and the weaving of cloth must also be credited to this ingenious people. Other tribes were also attracted by the comfort and security of life on the Nile, eventually absorbing the Badarian stock and at the same time catching the flicker of cultural light which they, in their turn, passed on to others.

Two waves of new peoples, one from Libya on the west, the

---

3. A good example of their drawings may be found in H. E. Winlock: *The Rise and Fall of the Middle Kingdom in Thebes,* New York, 1947, pp. 61–62, pl. 35.

other from the east, appeared in the valley in the course of the ensuing centuries. These pre-dynastic folk carried on where their predecessors had left off by making copper the basic metal for tools and weapons, by executing some fine vase-work in hard stone and constructing more elaborate tombs whose broken bones, however, echo some barbaric rite of neolithic ancestry. They worked toward the organization of the calendar, a system of time-reckoning based on the rising of Sirius in conjunction with that of the sun, which was not fully worked out until dynastic times. We can be thankful that these people, looking ahead so clearly into eternity, still found it necessary to set down definite limitations for time. And while it must have caused some confusion later on because of its inaccuracies, their calendar was far superior to the cumbersome version of Roman times.[4] It was during this period that the two kingdoms of the north and south were united into one nation, nominally by Menes, but judging from art objects and inscriptions, by several monarchs. For purposes of administration, the land was divided into what the Greeks later called nomes, an outgrowth of an earlier clan division. For the first time writing appears in the form of hieroglyphs as well as a more convenient system known as hieratic. A census or numbering of the people was taken at regular intervals, a valuable asset for establishing dates. All in all, considerable advance was made during these obscure ages, for when the light of self-consciousness dawned on the Old Kingdom, many a tradition and institution stood firmly rooted in a revered past.

The Old Kingdom, so-called, brings us face to face with a culture ripened to maturity, presided over by rulers and nobles whose feet were firmly planted in the moving sands of time, whose eyes seem fixed on a transparent vision of eternity. Zoser, assisted by his wise counsellor and architect, Imhotep, erected the first great pyramid as an eternal resting place for his mortal remains and left the kingdom better

---

4. O. Neugebauer (*The Exact Sciences in Antiquity*, Princeton, 1952, pp. 81–86) gives us the best summary of the Egyptian calendar and its advantages.

organized and unified than the political dream of Plato. This monarch, as well as his successor, Sneferu, made a number of conquests and expeditions into the borderlands of Egypt, bringing back gold and ivory from the south, malachite from Sinai, and cedars from the land of Syria; later pharaohs also brought incense, myrrh, and gums from Punt, the name of an unidentified land somewhere along the Red Sea coast.[5] Khufu, Khafre, and Menkure of the fourth dynasty, about whom Herodotus gives us fabulous tales, have left to the ages awe-inspiring monuments of their power in the form of pyramids, temples, the *mastabas* of their nobles, and the Sphinx. Pepi II, said to have reigned over ninety years, lived out the epilogue of Egypt's most glorious period of culture before time brought change and decay to the pharaoh and his administration, which had been an eternal fixity in the minds of the people. Throughout this era men lived and moved within the framework of institutions fashioned and sanctioned by the gods, the first rulers of the land who, when they retired to a remote region, left it in the care of a favored son. Egypt with its Nile had always been there; the pharaoh's good and wise rule was not to be questioned; the protection of the gods was assured in this world and the next. And why should posterity presume to make a change in what had been made well for now and forevermore? Small wonder that their statues look over and beyond us with such an air of defiant individualism and unshakeable self-confidence!

One can scarcely conceive of a time in history when the people and wealth of a nation, the resources of nature, the sanction of religion, coupled with the traditions of the past, lent more support to the arbitrary rule of a single man. He had his priests to render fitting service to the gods, his vizier to take care of the administration of the two kingdoms, his palace and harem to minister to his pleasure. His subjects paid their taxes in produce or in labor on his lands and on monuments to perpetuate his name; his scribe, an official of no mean rank, kept a record of all transactions and events of importance; the world's

---

5. P. Herrmann (*Conquest by Man,* New York, 1954, pp. 64ff.) suggests it was located on the Zambesi.

best architects, sculptors, and craftsmen, the most advanced tools, the most durable materials were at his disposal. Beyond his frontiers there was no nation to threaten his power. The peasant and artisan, at the base of the pyramid of power, lived and labored as if their part in life had been ordained by divine decree, and as long as they were assured of some measure of security in this life and the next, they were comparatively happy within the circumscribed area of their existence. Why should they complain when they enjoyed that very certainty and security mankind had been groping for through untold centuries? The man of low degree was, in one respect, no more hedged in by custom than the pharaoh, who, with all his might and wealth, was forced to submit to a monotonous routine every day of his life. Rigid, formal conformity was the price every Egyptian gladly paid for a happy sense of security. We think only of the boredom of such an existence, but for the pious Egyptian of that day an occasional spell of ennui was far better than the dangerous consequences of non-conformity.

Soon after Pepi II was laid to rest, the nobles, too powerful to be held down any longer by one man, broke up the unity of the kingdom and threw the country into political confusion. When order was once more restored in the time of Mentuhotep II, just prior to the twelfth dynasty, we find the land and its people, in spite of an apparent sameness on the surface, had taken on a different tone. There is no question that Senusert III was one of the greatest pharaohs of Egypt, a great conqueror, administrator and builder. The development of the Fayoum, the canal dug around the first cataract, the canal from the Nile delta to the Red Sea were great enterprises worthy of great men and far more humanitarian than the monumental achievements of the fourth dynasty. The labyrinth was one of the great marvels of the ancient world, but it was not put up as a glorification of a single man or god. The capital was transferred to Thebes, where Amon-Ra became the great national divinity, although the sentiments of the people were not attracted to such a political center of religion. The old forms were still strong enough to claim the allegiance of the populace, to offer a sense of security, and if we put too much faith in the boastings of pharaohs, the Middle Kingdom may appear to be a continuation of the Old. Beneath the surface, if we read between the lines of literature and observe their works of art, a new viewpoint was developing in the Egyptian mind, which brought with it a new consciousness of social relationships tempered by a more human perspective.

At the very outset of the twelfth dynasty, Amenemhet I, in a disillusioned piece of admonition, posthumously warned his son to trust no man once he was seated on the throne, a piece of advice inspired by a palace revolution in which the monarch probably lost his life. The pharaoh's words imply that if man is not to be trusted, he has at least attained a level where human worth, regardless of its rank in state or society, must be reckoned with. The romance of Sinuhe, the paintings on the walls of tombs, reflect pleasures of everyday life enjoyed as much for their human value as for what they might contribute to the well-being of a superior. Osiris, whose tomb became a popular religious center, took a personal interest in every man, high or low; priest, peasant, and potentate all appeared before his judgment seat in the next world. Although the noble saw the advantages of a more centralized government, he was not likely to allow the pharaoh to forget the lessons of the past. The pharaoh too seems more human in these times, somewhat less absorbed in eternity beyond time, more tolerant of the frailties of human nature. And yet the shadow of the past was so heavy over his eyes that the Egyptian was loath to let the human element break through the hard shell of tradition. Revolutions might come and go, but a feeling of security, for the citizen of Egypt, was worth more than the risks of individual freedom.

And then came the invasion, the first serious catastrophe suffered at the hands of a foreign power. With the aid of the horse and the chariot, new weapons of war in Africa, the Hyksos, so-called, conquered a good share of Egypt and ruled the country with a high hand from their capital in the delta. Not until Ahmose, the founder of the eighteenth dynasty, came to power, did his people make any headway against the invader;

they not only drove the enemy from the land but pursued him into Palestine. Now that the Egyptian had tasted the fruits of foreign conquest, he could no longer remain content within his own borders. The pharaohs, once more in full control of the government, not only ruled without the nomarchs who had lost their power under the Hyksos, but went on, as conquering generals, to master all of Syria. To be sure, Hatshepsut, the great queen of the empire, refrained from conquest while she built Egypt's most beautiful temple and despatched a profitable expedition to Punt, but her successor, Tuthmose III, led his armies through Syria to the other side of the Euphrates, thus enlarging the empire to its greatest extent in the history of Egypt. Amenhotep III, while he spent much time and money on building enterprises, was content, for the most part, to live a life of luxury with his queens, both native and foreign. Egypt was now a power to be reckoned with in the family of oriental nations.

At the apex of her power Egypt produced one of those enigmatic figures the world has never learned to appreciate fairly. Amenhotep IV, or Akhenaton, as he called himself, broke away from the priesthood of Thebes, and since religion and politics were so closely intertwined, he also severed connections with many political traditions of the past. Such a revolution in Egypt was, of course, more obvious on the side of religion whose gods and priesthoods he brushed aside in favor of his Aton, a single divine manifestation sustaining the world by his life-giving rays. On the political front the revolution was more passive, allowing the rich and hard-won empire to fall into neglect. Finding the atmosphere of Thebes far from congenial, the monarch, his family, and his court removed to the modern Tell el-Amarna. While Akhenaton built up his new city and established his new divinity in an appropriate setting of ritual and worship, the Hittites in the north, despite all the complaints of faithful governors, duped Akhenaton grossly at his own court until nearly all Syria was lost. At the close of his reign the priesthood of Thebes, taking advantage of the weakness of his heirs and playing on the popular sentiment in favor of empire, snuffed out the new movement with a vengeance born of religious hatred. The royal family once more took up its residence in the old capital and left el 'Amarna a colorful dream on the encrusted surface of tradition.

It took some time before subsequent rulers were able to regain some of their lost territories. Once the kingdom at home was made secure, Seti I and Rameses II led their troops against the Hittites in the north; Rameses II, after winning a questionable victory at Kadesh, concluded a non-aggression pact with his enemy and returned home to live out his reign as the most vain, pompous, and splendor-loving pharaoh Egypt had ever known. However, neither the Hittites nor the Egyptians were destined to offer the other any aid in a later invasion by strange peoples from the north. Apparently they overran the heart of the Hittite kingdom and then knocked at the gates of Egypt, where they were repulsed on land and sea by Rameses III; he managed to preserve Egypt intact, but Syria was lost forever. In the meantime, the priesthood of Amon, which had grown apace in wealth and prestige, gained such a hold on the throne that eventually the priests were able to exercise full control of the generals raised to the apex of power. They could not, on the other hand, check the crumbling of the political structure and gave way in turn to invading Libyans and Ethiopians and finally to the powerful army of Essarhaddon. Egypt's long career as an independent power was almost over.

The empire brought untold wealth to the country, including luxuries carried over the sea and along trade routes from the east. The pharaohs, now undisputed owners of the land, were no longer vexed by noblemen, and consequently they were, in a sense, a step further removed from the people as a whole. Young men from Syria were trained and saturated with Egyptian ideals before they were sent back to govern their native provinces, a custom which insured a measure of loyalty to their masters, but the Egyptian himself showed no great enthusiasm for taking up arms to fight in behalf of the empire; he was now no more of a soldier than before, and since soldiers were needed now more than ever, the mercenary took his place in the ranks.

The pharaohs set up great monuments to honor their names; they spent stupendous sums on the priesthood and shrines of Amon, the state god of the land, a divinity somewhat removed from the Isis and Osiris of the middle classes and far above the peasant of the soil. Despite the new contacts with lands beyond the borders, which should have developed a more international viewpoint, the incubus of the state religion, except for the reign of Akhenaton, continued to sap the strength of the land, and when Egypt could give no more, the cult of Amon still hemmed her in like a desiccated coral reef around a Pacific isle.

Egyptian religion, as is the case with so many oriental peoples, was the most permeating influence in life, and therefore it absorbed the rights of philosophy and speculative science almost completely, it molded government throughout Egypt's history, and it dictated most of the norms of art production. Nowhere in ancient times were the traditions and conventions of a people more permanently fixed by the scruples of religion. Once in control of the helm, this powerful agent of subjective desire squelched any possibility of scepticism so necessary for the development of independent thought. In a sense, the pattern of living was prescribed for every Egyptian by religious formula, a pattern whose color and shading were supplied by the demands he levied on his environment from birth to the grave. All this was somehow worked into ritual to which the individual clung as closely as the river to its channel. Already grown to full stature at the dawn of history, religion reveals little direct evidence about its origin, but when we consider how certain phenomena in Egyptian life operated with almost clocklike regularity—the rising and ebbing of the Nile, the coming of day and night—we can understand how the sameness of the desert and sky, added to the dependability of natural processes, gave the native a foretaste of eternity and immortality in the present. It is because this sameness contributed so much to hard and fast rules in religious tradition that animal forms, so frequently lopped off elsewhere in the early history of religion, were still attached to divine images in the later period of enlightenment.

Where the modern individual finds freedom in the privilege of dissenting and revolting against usage, the Egyptian found his highest fulfillment within the masonry of conformity.

Like so many institutions of the Nile-dweller the total manifestations of religious worship took on the form of a pyramidal hierarchy. Viewed from the top, one might call it originally and predominantly monotheistic, while from the standpoint of regional cults, it is unmistakably polytheistic in character. From other angles it might be called theistic or pantheistic, but none of these terms, I dare say, were valid for the Egyptian, for, in the first place, it was the only religion he recognized as such and so it had no comparative value; in the second place, when he was absorbed in the worship of one divinity, he regarded this divinity as the one and all or, in our language, one of the numerous manifestations of the supreme power. Nor was there any perceptible gap between the reality of the concrete and the ideal. In fact, if there is a distinctive feature in this religion, it is a materialistic basis for both its highest and lowest manifestations. The life of the gods, the career of man in the next world, if we may judge from the tomb paintings, are derived from the physical life of man and his native environment.

Abstractions, then, found less expression in Egyptian life and religion than among other peoples. The sun god, exalted as he was above many others, maintained his role as divine boatman moving across the sky from east to west; Osiris, for all his career in popular mythology, preserved his connection with the Nile and the fertilization of the soil; nowhere do we hear of anything divine similar to the Roman concepts of concord and peace. On the other hand, we have no right to deny the Egyptian the use of symbols, but unlike so many others, he possessed the happy faculty of making divine attributes real and symbolic at the same time. Where in the history of art can one find anything more alive than the falcon of Old Kingdom statuary, anything as alert as the eye of Horus or as feline as the Egyptian cat? Religion, here as elsewhere, had its symbols and sublimations, but on the Nile, it always carried with it something of the richness, the freshness of immediately apprehended reality.

The Nile and the sun, the two great benefactors in the life of the native, played the major roles in their hierarchy of divinity, and as a proper balance between the two was necessary for the support of life, the priests of each cult, though they were keen rivals, were forced to acknowledge the power of both gods. Thus there were two versions of after-life: one associated with the sun and its bark making the journey across the sky and the other in the kingdom of Osiris, who borrowed a number of features earlier attached to the sun god. The pharaoh and his family were recognized as the heirs of the sun, while the people of the middle class, especially in the Middle Kingdom, were stronger devotees of the Osiris cult. Likewise, both the sun god and Osiris were said, according to their advocates, to have ruled over the land before the pharaohs. The boat of the sun, somewhat out of place in the sky, suggests an original identity or close connection with the god of the river, but of this there is no mention.

The creation of the world and its divinities, despite the occasional confusion of names, can be traced rather clearly. In the beginning, if we may use such a term, there was only an indeterminate, chaotic mass containing a potentially creative principle called Kheperi or Atum; as a self-created, immortal being he is often symbolized by the scarab, a creature the Egyptians mistakenly thought endowed with similar powers of self-creation. This god brought about a division between heat, Shu, and moisture, Tefnut. Shu, the god of heat and atmosphere, and his wife, Tefnut the goddess of coolness and moisture, brought forth Geb, the god of the earth, and Nut, the goddess of the sky. In popular representation we find a personification of Shu, the atmosphere, standing on the earth and holding up the star-studded body of Nut on his hands, a group reminiscent of the Greek Atlas supporting the weight of the world. The sun god Ra, already potentially existent and sometimes identified with Kheperi, now finds room for the exercise of his functions and assumes concrete form, sailing across the sky from sunrise to sunset. Geb and Nut, in turn, bring forth Osiris and his great sister and wife, Isis, Set and Nephthys.

According to one legend, the sun god Ra was once a ruler of mankind, but being dissatisfied with the behavior of his subjects, whom he had created, he exterminated all but a few of them and transferred his abode to the sky. The storm clouds and the rain were his great foes, whose opposition, when we consider the scanty rainfall in Egypt, appears to be a neligible factor; when, however, a heavy rain came, the people were so poorly prepared it left devastation in its wake. The pharaoh reigned over the land as the representative and son of the sun god, which means that his priesthood became powerful enough in early times to place one of their number on the throne. Alexander the Great, after his conquest of Egypt, bowed before this age-old belief when he made his pilgrimage to the shrine of Amon in the desert to be declared a rightful descendant of the pharaohs and the divinity. Both the obelisk and the pyramid, as is commonly known, are symbols of the sun god. Many of the monarchs of the Old Kingdom were especially devoted to his worship, to which their names and pyramids bear ample testimony. Buried within these monuments, which they hoped would endure through time and eternity, their apices greeting the first rays of the sun before they were visible to the common man below, the pharaoh could feel himself, in a sense, reunited with his divine father.

Osiris, the god of the Nile and the champion of the middle and lower classes, became especially popular in the Middle Kingdom, perhaps because his story was more human in its appeal than that of the sun god; moreover, wealth sufficient to erect a mortuary monument was not a prerequisite to enter his realm after death. Osiris and his sister-wife, Isis, as rulers of Egypt, had integrated the land and then civilized it in spite of Set, their evil brother of the desert who wished to deprive Osiris of his kingdom. According to Plutarch, who recorded the story for the Greek and Roman world, Set fashioned a chest large enough to contain the body of his brother. Persuading Osiris by means of a ruse to lie down in the chest, he clamped down the lid and threw the chest into the Nile. It was also said that he cut the body in pieces and scattered them to the four winds. Like Ceres searching for her lost daughter, Isis wandered over the face of the earth until she found her husband and restored him to life with the aid of Thoth, whom we shall mention later. In the meantime, Set had usurped his brother's throne while Osiris became ruler of the world below, and Isis brought forth a son she called Horus, whom, to elude the watchful eye of Set, she reared in the marshes of the delta. Horus, borrowed by the cult of Osiris from the myth of the sun god, waxed strong enough under his mother's care to engage the wicked Set in battle; once defeated, the villain was duly punished, and Horus, as well as his mother, took a prominent place in the Osirian kingdom of the lower world.

It is no difficult matter to recognize in this tale another myth of regeneration, first inspired by the change of seasons and later woven into a story of human and religious significance, a process common to so many early peoples. Osiris, the traditional god of the Nile and hence of vegetation watered by that river, was hard-pressed each year by Set, a god removed from the sky where, as the enemy of the sun god, he symbolized darkness. As the enemy of the Nile he no doubt represented the desert. Horus, as we pointed out, was also removed from the story of Ra to play his dramatic role in a new setting. The family devotion between husband and wife, between mother and son, the path of filial duty trod by Horus in avenging his father made a strong enough impression on the common man not only to inspire a like behavior among members of the same family but to consider the rewards of such behavior a compensation for a life of honest toil. The latter were more than willing to identify their careers with the divine family to reap the inheritance of the just. The movement was evidently powerful enough to be free from the oppression of the other cult and sincere enough to establish a shrine at Abydos, supposedly the site of Osiris' tomb, where his whole drama was presented in much the same way as the mysteries at Eleusis or the passion play in modern Germany.

A large part of the Egyptians' literature, in fact most of their religious thinking, revolved around life after death, and everything possible was done to insure a safe arrival at the final haven. In keeping with the two major myths there were also two versions of life hereafter, both employing certain divinities in common, the sun god being the central figure in the one and Osiris in the other. After the proper ceremonies had been performed by the priest at the tomb, the pharaoh, as the descendant of the sun god, first submitted to a purification by holy water, then set out on his journey to the east, a full account of which is set forth in the *Pyramid Texts*. Three major obstacles beset the path of the traveler: a sea over which he must be ferried, the ascent by ladder to the sky, and the gateway to the realm of divine blessedness. If the ferryman, the gatekeeper, or the sun god himself should not comply with the requests of the newcomer, magic supplied him with passwords to remove all resistance. To one familiar with the personal God of Christianity, it seems strange that the humble suppliant at the gates of the hereafter should reveal himself more powerful than the sun god or threaten him to gain his ends, but we must remember that, to the Egyptian, the next life was a literal transcription, in many respects, of the here and now, and so the pharaoh must retain certain prerogatives of a ruler; it will be recalled, too, that Ra was also an earthly ruler before his ascent to the sky. Aristocracy was as divine as divinity itself.

Once admitted to the inner circle of the gods, the pharaoh takes his place in the boat of Ra to sail across the sky from east to west, still a monarch exercising sovereign sway and at the same time free from many of the limitations of the finite. Nevertheless, while his freedom from death, age, and the effects of the passing years is repeatedly emphasized, the fear of hunger and thirst renders his heaven a curious mélange of the finite and infinite. The offerings presented at the tomb are somehow transported to the sky, and magic again comes to the rescue, if the gods should prove recalcitrant. The serpent of the earth must also be guarded against—and all this despite the mystic union the deceased has achieved with the sun god. Like so many divinities who grow impatient with their self-sufficiency, the pharaoh issues his commands in terms of both the finite and infinite to guarantee his continuity and magnify his glory. On the whole, this absorbing and selfish desire to banish death from human perspective had created an egocentric ruler with little more to do than to impress his importance on his environment, all of which, from our viewpoint, is almost devoid of human interest. This failing was made up for, to a certain extent, by the hereafter presided over by Osiris.

This realm, referred to as below the earth and open to every man and woman regardless of rank or vocation, is described for us not only in literature but also on an illustrated papyrus relating the experiences of a certain Ani and his wife before they achieve salvation. The pair, long forewarned about their obligations, are brought before the scales of judgment presided over by the jackal-headed Anubis and Thoth, who functions as the recording scribe. The deceased must make what is known as the "Negative Confession," in which he denies being guilty of such sins as murder, lying, excessive pride, infliction of pain, ambition, disregard for the needs of the poor, and others we might consider insignificant. Having satisfied the forty-two judges and having seen the heart on one side of the scale balance the feather on the other side, the deceased breathes more freely, and the monster, waiting all this time behind Thoth to devour the wicked, is dismissed. Horus, the son of Osiris, then leads Ani by the hand into the presence of his enthroned father and the goddesses Isis and Nephthys, where Ani presents his offerings and is justified. But before he can enter the realm of the blessed and taste the waters of the celestial Nile, he must pass through a number of gateways guarded by divine doorkeepers; in each case he must be ready with a correct reply to every question, information which every Egyptian could find in the *Book of the Dead*. Throughout the whole proceeding it was highly important to adhere strictly to the ritual prescribed by religious tradition.

Along with the desire to submerge the fact of death in a continued life in the hereafter, this people lay claim to a highly developed moral consciousness, but actually their reliance on magic was a hindrance in this respect. There is no indication that they were aware of the paradox inherent in the concept of a good god who allows evil to interfere with his program, because their gods were not exclusively good, but they were concerned about the difference between right and wrong, for the latter set obstacles in the way of man both here and in the next world. That "the good men do lives after them" seemed to bear fruit even for the pharaoh, who had to be justified in the sight of the sun god. The "Negative Confession" before the judgment seat of Osiris is even more explicit in its details. On the other hand, we wonder how much weight it all carried when magic was capable of meeting all these difficulties.[6] In the good old days, when the gods ruled over the earth, there was no death, no murder, no crime of any kind, men were told, implying that men had no need to look forward to a relief in the next world. When we examine the facts in the light of so many noble claims to a moral consciousness recorded in the tombs, we realize what a gap lay between what they wanted to be (and perhaps what they believed they were) and what they actually were in practice. The most binding seals, the most threatening curses, and magical formulae, however forceful, were of no more avail against the tomb robber than against the modern archaeologist.

Now that we know something of his claims to the hereafter, the focal point of his ambitions, in what form, we may ask, did the Egyptian survive after death? The manifestation of the personality, the ba, took on the form of a human-headed bird, although we may be sure that, if we may judge from mortuary paintings, the dead were also pictured in the bodies they had possessed in life. It is important to remember that the ba was not a part of man in this life but was called into being after death. Another manifestation, perhaps more essential to his spiritual welfare and more like his earthly body in appearance, was the ka or double, separated from man in this life but generally united with him in the next, where it watched over him like a guardian genius. The ka, or vital force, could, if it wished, put

6. Many writers fail to recognize the nullifying effect of magic on moral values. Cf. H. W. Smith: *Man and His Gods*, Boston, 1953, pp. 112-14.

on the material form of the body and eat and drink like any earthly organism; every Egyptian was concerned about how his ka would recognize its counterpart in the beyond. It could also enter into a statue; hence such an image of the deceased was placed in the tomb for the sake of the ka's identification with a concrete representation of the dead man. There was also a "shining spirit" and a shadow, which, although attached to the body in life, lingered after death near the tomb like our prowling ghost. The ren, or name, must be protected lest an enemy, by learning it, gain a certain magic power over the dead man; for the gods it was an Achilles' heel by means of which the pharaoh could bend them to his will. The ib was the heart, the seat of the conscience, the will, and thought. After trying to disentangle the various manifestations of his personality one might well believe in the heart as the source of the Egyptian's religious thinking.

Other forces also play a prominent role in Egyptian religion. Aside from the local divinities of the nomes and cities, great reverence was attached to Ptah, worshipped especially at Memphis as the patron of the artists, the master architect and creator of the world. Closely associated with him was the ibis-headed Thoth, the divine mind, the master of the word and hence the patron of the scribes; he it was whose words had revived the dead Osiris, who stood beside the scales of justice in the lower world, recording the results; he it was who, as the lord of the written word, had handed down to mankind books on ritual, education, and the sciences. Anubis, the jackal-headed divinity, also attended the scales of justice with Thoth; he was the master of mummification, for it was this god who had preserved the body of Osiris by his peculiar art. Isis, the goddess of fertility, appears in various guises in different localities: at Denderah she was identified with Hathor, the cow goddess; at Bubastis she appeared as Bast, the divine cat; at Sais the Libyans identified her with their goddess Neit, the goddess of war; and at Memphis she took on the form of a lioness. The associations with the animal world had been sanctioned by the earliest Egyptians and preserved intact throughout the later centuries.

Amon-Ra, a synthesis of the sun god and a local divinity, became the state divinity when the pharaohs set up their residence in Thebes. Amon, originally an obscure local god, was solarized by his association with Ra, the combination reaching such a height of sublimation it threw the other divinities into the shade, while the god's priesthood became the virtual dictator in religious affairs in the land. But he always was and remained a national god; as the armies of Tuthmose III moved beyond the Nile valley to the banks of the Euphrates some men must have realized, without daring to express themselves openly, how inadequately the old religion met the challenge of empire. A heresy, if we may call it such, grew in time, cropping out subtly in the worship of Amon, until Akhenaton, the most controversial figure in Egyptian history, was able to make a break with the past. At first it appeared no more startling than the introduction of a new god into an already crowded pantheon, but evidently Amon would make little compromise; consequently the pharaoh, a man of strong convictions, broke sharply with the Theban priesthood, forsook the old capital for another site and built a new city, which we know as el 'Amarna, for his court and new divinity. Henceforth he was an ardent crusader for a new religion, obliterating the name of Amon on all monuments in favor of Aton, the universal god upon whom he showered all his devotion.

And what was the nature of this god who called forth so much enthusiasm from one man and aroused so much enmity in others? Judging from the art of the el 'Amarna period, he was the sun god dressed in a new form, the emphasis being placed on the life-giving disc. Again and again we see this pharaoh raising his hands in adoration of this disc from which rays, culminating in outstretched hands, extend on all sides. He could not have made a happier choice for a symbol than these hands stemming from the source of all life and embracing everything within reach with a beneficent gesture; the hands also contributed to make the god more human in nature. Gone was the bark of Ra, Amon, the myth of Osiris and the gods sanctioned by time and tradition in favor of a more universal divinity, more materialistic, more naturalistic in his manifestations. From the hymns of Akhenaton we learn something more tangible about him; he is described as "lord of eternity," "living in truth," "the only god," the creator of all life whose rays extend out over the green sea, over lands beyond Egypt, who made other peoples different and caused them to speak with different tongues, the god of all waters, plants, animals, and men. There is the same relationship as before between the supreme deity as father and the pharaoh, but now it is established on a more intimate, affectionate, and human basis. Without a doubt it was a new conception of divinity in the orient, inspired by a broader feeling of toleration toward all mankind and more concerned with the natural evidence for the god's power in creation. We can easily understand why the king's contemporaries, in a land where difference of belief in religion spelled enmity, fell so far short of comprehending its significance.

What manner of character was this Akhenaton, the creator of the new universal sun god? Some have put him down as a fanatical reformer, and no doubt he appeared in that light to his contemporary opponents, but were not so many of the oriental leaders fanatical in defending a belief or cause? Some dismiss him as one who adapted religion to a broader political horizon, but if he was interested only in turning religion into a political channel, why did he so obviously neglect the political aspect of the empire? He was not so much an exception that he was not an Egyptian; he was also more than an Egyptian. He was such in that he worshipped a sun god in his concrete manifestations and identified himself as the son of his god; he was more than an Egyptian in that he saw the deficiencies of the old gods and possibly of their priesthoods as well. His was a vision of a greater world in which his god stepped over national boundaries to transcend all the petty differences of local religions. He was a genius in our sense of the term; hence the one-sidedness of his enthusiasm. Had he lived in the modern age, he might have been a poet of nature, a pantheist. Like Job, he gave expression to truths his own time could hardly appreciate and which later centuries were destined to restore with a more balanced evaluation in the scheme of things.

Once Akhenaton was in his tomb, his religion passed through a rapid epilogue. Since the reformer had no male issue and his successors were weak, the priests of Amon, having reasserted themselves by moving the capital back to Thebes, levelled el 'Amarna to the ground and restored their god to a position of greater prominence than before; Akhenaton became the criminal of the past and el 'Amarna an evil memory. But even Amon was forced to submit to a compromise not so apparent on the surface: a certain universality and a tendency toward a fusion with other deities can only be interpreted as a movement already initiated in a preceding period; the aloofness of the state god was somewhat moderated to a more spiritual communion with the lower classes similar to that enjoyed by the worshipper of Osiris in the Middle Kingdom. Magic, the handmaid of the desire for certainty, was restored to its place to stop up the gaps of any possible doubt; the old rituals and texts were imitated and copied by men who revered the word but had forgotten much of the meaning. The priesthood, by extending its sway over the political realm, eventually brought the state to ruin and then laid its own stagnant body on the burning pyre. After the inroads of foreigners, other gods lifted up their heads, while only Isis and Osiris were privileged to bask in the afterglow Egypt spread abroad through the Roman empire.

Both the spoken and the written word were generally held in high respect everywhere in the orient, perhaps because, like the monuments of stone, words inscribed in memory or on tablets snatched another segment from the ever-changing cosmos and reduced it to something approaching the eternal, the immutable. In Egypt too "the word was with God" and a powerful agent in the control of god and man. The words written on stone preserved the memory of a pharaoh's deed; the word of a magician cured the sick; the word of a priest swayed the will of the gods; it was the spoken word of Thoth that had revived the

slain Osiris. We refer to Egyptian characters as hieroglyphics,
which means sacred carvings. By means of the word the gods
made known their will to men, and in the same way men
communicated this meaning to others of a later time. Like a
divinity descending from heaven to earth it was a manifestation
of the formless in form, of the timeless and intangible in concrete
experience.

Records, which played no minor role in Egyptian life, were
written on stone, clay, wood, leather, and papyrus. Stone there
was aplenty; clay could be found and baked very easily; but
papyrus, the most convenient of all materials, required special
preparation. The stems of the plant, once they had been
gathered from the swamp, were cut into thin strips and laid side
by side on a flat surface; another row of strips was then laid
crosswise on the first, after which the rows were pressed
together, with the aid of a binding material, to form a sheet.
It was then ready for the scribe or for export to a foreign land.
The work of the scribe was held in high respect both by the
nobility and the common people. The man in authority who
desired to have records of his achievements made, the pharaohs
who required written statements of all administrative transactions, could hardly dispense with the ubiquitous recorder
standing ready with pencil and tablet. The lower classes realized
it was practically the only way the common man could rise
from the drudgery of manual labor to a position of respected
standing; one could become a pharaoh, a noble, a priest, and
inherit property by right of birth, but anyone with the ability
and industry to learn could attend a school for scribes. Parents
and elders exhorted the young to be diligent in acquiring wisdom, and a good part of wisdom was the almost magical ability
to record hieroglyphs legibly and artistically.

In school the aspiring youngster was taught both by flogging
and repeated admonishment. The animal in man, it was thought,
must be trained like the horse and dog, but since man was also
endowed with a mind, verbal admonition also had its place.
First the student had to learn how to draw the characters, then
he was given assignments to copy on the pages of a notebook,

a great number of which have come down to us. Egyptian writing is not as ideographic as the cuneiform of Babylon, nor is it alphabetic like our own; it is both ideographic and phonetic in character, consisting of stylized pictures of birds, animals, and objects familiar to Egyptian daily life. A more flowing and abbreviated form, known as hieratic, doubtless invented for the convenience of the business man, was developed along with a more popular version called demotic. To the artist these hieroglyphs or pictographs, already fully developed at the dawn of history, were of such decorative beauty as to be suitable for the embellishment of an architectural façade. How did we learn to decipher these characters? During the Napoleonic expedition to the land of the Nile, an inscription, recorded in Egyptian and Greek in the days of the Ptolemies, was found in the Rosetta section of the delta and later deciphered by the French scholar Champollion. The Rosetta Stone has been our chief asset in reading records of Egyptian history and literature.

As in all phases of his culture we find religion permeating a good share of the Egyptian's literature, especially the hymns of praise directed to the divinity. To create an atmosphere of awe before an overpowering deity, the poet resorts to certain stock phrases used over and over again, phrases common in the religious writings of so many nations and which tend to bore rather than elevate the modern reader. The sun god is described as self-begotten, the creator of heaven and earth, the lord of all things who drives away the darkness, fills the heart of every creature with joy, beats down his enemies, brings rejoicing to the gods in his bark, and rises in triumph each morning in the east to shower the land with his blessings. Any of the major divinities, especially the pharaoh, might be addressed as the lord of the two lands, the delight and joy of his worshippers, great in renown and honor; then follow various incidents in his history and references to his shrines and special benefits to mankind. Occasionally, the divinity is brought down to a more finite level where we can appreciate his more human aspects, where nature at large joins hands with the poet in a song of praise, *e.g.*, the soaring of the hawk, the power of the bull, the happy chattering of baboons at the rising of the sun are used as similes. This is especially true of the time of Akhenaton, who, in exalting the sun-disc, invites all nature to join in his rapture.

One of the hymns is a remarkable culmination of this type of literary effort in that it preserves all the dignity of ancient forms, while at the same time the imagination of the writer endows the lines with the quickening pulse of nature's dynamic forces; one is quick to respond to the electric charge emanating from the source of life in the sun's rays to the chick who "comes forth to chirp and walk on two legs." The powers of all the varied manifestations of divinity, casting aside their evil ways, are made to coalesce in the sun's disc, whence they spread abroad their beneficence to all creatures of the universe, including men of different race and color. In this Egyptian hymn there is a majestic cadence, a balance of structure, a simplicity of diction amounting to an act of purification on a higher plane than that scaled by the Aristotelian interpretation of tragedy. It has something of the parallelism of the Hebrew psalm, the second line echoing the first from the distant wall of the universe, although it has little of the other's lofty, resounding metaphor. Being conservative in style, the hymn has a certain compactness, is sparing of words to the extent that a single phrase or line can effectively paint an emotional canvas, delineate the outlines of character, or drive home some truth of cosmic significance. As the painter presents the body from more than one angle, the writer has reduced the whole man, intellectual and emotional, to a form prescribed by geometric law. The word, like the hieroglyph to the scribe, was a living symbol in the mind of the writer.

Another collection of writings, perhaps as old as the first scribe, is embodied in the *Pyramid Texts,* which the Egyptian held in high regard. While they trace their beginnings to a period before recorded history, they were supplemented in later times by men with a changed outlook and allegiance in matters divine, and in the days of the empire the inevitable commentator added his glosses, which were meant to clarify original meanings, but which, to us, only tend to jumble the text and confuse the reader. The later Egyptians, for the most part, had forgotten the meaning of the original and often copied the text verbatim from age to age. The *Book of the Dead*, a later development, was intended to serve as a guide through the pitfalls of the next world, and since it was molded by the dictates of magic, it also coerced the will of divinity to suit the desire of man. In early Egyptian history there was a strong emphasis on Ra and the sky over which he was lord, but in the Middle Kingdom the story of Osiris takes precedence; in fact there are passages where the latter's name was evidently substituted for that of another without considering the import of the text. The result of all this interpolation, for the modern, is a jumbled mass of prayer, magic, and wishful thinking as devoid of any common sense thinking as the *Enneads* of Plotinus or medieval science. Taken as a whole, these writings represent the Egyptian's subjective point of view at its best. More than sure that what he hoped for was just and predestined, mortal man talked to his god as a child dictates to her doll, plugging desperately all the holes through which the god might escape from his bidding. The texts were copied on papyrus, even on the interiors of coffins, and buried with the deceased to insure a life of blessings in the next world.

To strengthen himself against the enemies of darkness and to obtain his ends from the gods, the dead king identifies himself with creatures he believed the god had used for manifestation or whose ways man construed as being symbolic of divine power, and thus the pharaoh invested himself with the god's various powers. In one passage he is a bull who lords it over the field of the bull. He has kissed the sky like a hawk; he has leaped toward the sky like a grasshopper; he has cackled like a goose and alighted like a bird beside the divine clouds and the great dew. The subject entreats with humility; he prays with conviction; he threatens the god with the utterance of his sacred name; and in certain cases he devours the god to appropriate his powers. He calls himself Osiris, Anubis, Horus, and Kheperi; in the fields of Hetep he wants to eat, drink, plough, reap, fight, make love, never to be a slave and always to have authority. In one breath he says: "Thy will be done" and compels the powers that be to submit to his own will. This may have been good poetry to the ancients, and because we know so little about their metrical systems, we cannot pass judgment. As far as magic is concerned, who are we to throw a stone, who tell God in our prayers how to run the universe to our best advantage?

Another category of literature includes the proverbs or admonitions supposedly handed down by the wise men of the Old Kingdom and cherished as pearls of wisdom by all who sought social or political advancement. Ptahhotep and Kagemni had climbed the ladder of success within certain limitations, which means they had found favor in the eyes of the pharaoh; they were in a position to counsel others with advice destined to become, for the Egyptians, as eternal as the pyramids. In accordance with the Egyptian viewpoint, the author avoids the abstract in favor of the concrete and practical; he is concerned not so much with virtue as its own reward as with the impression one makes on others, especially superiors.[7] One is told how to conduct himself at table, when to keep silent, to avoid arrogance, greed, and chattering, to be a good example for others, and above all, to fear, love, and obey those in authority. Like so many orientals, the Egyptian sage believed that fear should precede love in the human heart.[8] There is here, as in the *Proverbs* of the Hebrews, a compactness of style, a tendency to drive straight to the point from a number of angles; moreover, at the end of an admonition there is either a strong contrast or a compelling picture to sum up the lesson. The third party in

---

7. W. M. Flinders Petrie: *Religion and Conscience in Ancient Egypt*, London, 1920, p. 77.

8. The following passage has been quoted by H. Frankfort *op. cit.*, p. 108:

> Let there be terror of me like the terror of thee.
> Let there be fear of me like the fear of thee.
> Let there be awe of me like the awe of thee.
> Let there be love of me like the love of thee.

authority, however, who sees and approves right conduct, is always necessary to complete the scene, if such maxims of Polonius are to have any value. There is in this literature as much, if not more, expediency than in the writings of Francis Bacon and Benjamin Franklin.

Fancy was given a loose reign in the colorful romance, in tales of adventure, and stories of magic, all of which are fully as marvellous as later oriental tales more familiar to the modern reader. The account of Prince Charming, fated to fall a prey to an animal, who wins his bride in spite of obstacles, reads like a *Märchen* of the Grimm brothers; the ship-wrecked sailor, like an ancient Sinbad, survives the perils of a stormy sea before a huge but kindly serpent comes to his rescue on a lonesome isle; a magician, performing in the presence of Khufu, severs the head of an animal and then restores it to its place, all of which serves as a prelude to a melancholy prophecy for the king; a jewel lost in a lake is brought back by a wonder-worker who rolls up one side of the lake on the other in much the same way as the Red Sea was parted by Moses. Anpu and Bata, at the outset, play their parts in the Egyptian version of the tale of Potiphar's wife before ascending to a divine level for further, more fanciful, adventures. Apart from a vague moral atmosphere, the bulk of the tales, of which a number are incomplete, are pure flights of fancy, devoid of system or reason. Obviously they were meant to be recited for entertainment, and therefore much depended on a narrator capable of enhancing, by word of mouth, the marvels of the story. If this is so, it lends a measure of truth to the story by Plato about Thoth and the introduction of letters into Egypt.[9] These tales, as we read them today, lose much of their charm, and the characters, saturated as they are with magic, are little more than figures in a puppet show.

One tale, because it shows no trace of magic and probably has a historical background, makes a valuable contribution to the Egyptian viewpoint. Sinuhe, a man of some consequence at a twelfth dynasty court, flees his country out of fear lest he be

---

9. *Phaedrus,* 274c.

identified as an accomplice in a plot against the new pharaoh about to take over the reins of power. In a foreign land he ingratiates himself with the king, takes on foreign customs and manners, and is given a wife and land; his prowess and strength as a fighter also add considerable prestige to his name. He lives in high honor until he reaches old age, when a yearning for his homeland prompts him to write to the pharaoh, the same ruler he had fled from. The latter, ready to forget the past, receives him back home with a welcome gesture. In a new home, especially built for the fugitive, he passes the balance of his days in happiness. The modern reader would naturally be curious about the family Sinuhe left behind, but the Egyptian brushes it aside as of no importance. After all, Sinuhe was back home where he was assured a proper burial and a glorious life beyond! And so the story ends as it should end.

In times of adversity men were, as now, wont to complain about their loss of fortune. During the decline of Greek civilization, the thinker either sought salvation in terms of the inner man or turned to a fuller exploitation of material pleasures, but in Egypt, where inner security was the norm, he had no recourse to stoicism; his bitterness was so much more pronounced, his despair more suicidal or his wantonness more emphatic, just because his inner stability had been rudely shaken. We have two excellent examples in Egyptian literature: the dialogue between a man and his soul which harks back to the period of unrest between the Old and Middle Kingdoms,[10] and the *Song of the Harper,* composed some time after the breakup of the twelfth dynasty.[11] The repetition of the opening line, in the first example, sustains and intensifies the emotion, like the beating of tom-toms, until the concentrated desire of the poet, wrested by the weight of calamity from its anchor of certainty, burns every bridge behind him as it saturates his outlook with despairing colors and marches on to inevitable self-destruction. The harper, like Omar of the Persians, mocks at the sameness of things in

---

10. J. Baikie: *A History of Egypt,* London, 1929, Vol. I, p. 363.
11. H. E. Winlock: *op. cit.,* p. 121.

a tone of irony, although in his glorification of the transient there is a nostalgic sadness which draws on our sympathy. These poems are not mere expressions of disappointment over political upsets; they are not songs of self-commiseration in the narrow sense of the term. When we consider that the pharaoh and his power was the connecting link between the divine and the secular, the past and the future, and the arbiter over the powers of nature, a political disaster loomed up as a major threat to the whole cosmos, including man, and so when our poet turns his back on the past his lines carry much more weight than the wistful sadness of Horace.[12]

The earliest lyrics and love songs in the history of literature were composed by Egyptians. These lines are as telling in their effect and as delicate as those defining a figure in their best painting, as elegant and sensitive as the features of Nefertiti; they can be familiar without being sloppy, frank in their materialism and, as in their sculpture, they can raise the commonplace to the dignity of eternity. A certain crystalline clarity, like that of a Mozart sonata, is so apparent to the reader that one suspects the poet, now and then, of false modesty. Poetry was the mirror in which he saw the divinity of things more clearly, and this divinity was more clear in the human sphere than elsewhere.

Although the types of literature composed on the banks of the Nile will bear comparison with those of the later European, many subjects which we take for granted were completely ignored by the Egyptians. Tragedy was certainly as common in their life as for the Greek of Sophocles' time, but why is it so glaringly absent in their writings? As we have seen in the tale of Sinuhe, they were conscious of the foreigner beyond their borders, yet they paid no attention to his history; in fact the history of their own land was vague to the later Egyptians and suffered from a lack of comparative values. We miss the curiosity which creates a system of philosophy to explain the phenomena of the cosmos and we see little interest in any kind of science

---

12. *Odes,* II, 3.

for its own sake. Why is there no biography or autobiography? We know the pharaohs by their portraits and achievements in military campaigns and great monuments, but the intimate pictures and foibles of their personalities, as we construe this term, are not to be found. Why has the Egyptian left us no law code? Since all these questions are bound up with his viewpoint, it would be out of place to explore them until we have taken a glimpse at his art.

The Egyptian was little more interested in art as an aesthetic experience than was the primitive. Both regarded it as a means to a practical end, in which capacity it was either substituted for magic or identified with it, but, for the Egyptian, the purpose of art was no longer the attainment of immediate ends; it served largely to guarantee continued satisfaction and pleasure in another world. Beyond the fact that it had to reflect man's most urgent desires, it required no justification in theory, no apologist to defend its media or methods. The appearance of the subject in objective form was subservient to the dictates of religion, which means it was consistently conservative, for ritual, in which religion expressed its aim, often enlisted art in its service and employed the same motives, forms, and symbols through successive generations. Art was, then, the handmaid of a very strict taskmaster. The artist, in such a program, had no personality in our sense of the term. Where he is mentioned, his name and achievements, like puppets in a theatre, reflect the glory of his lord more than his own individual contribution.

Already at the beginning of the Old Kingdom the Egyptian was concerned with the tomb, his eternal dwelling-place. Since life in the beyond was a close facsimile of his present existence, it was necessary to preserve the body as well as its belongings, an urge which called for the elaborate process of mummification. The grave too was enclosed with masonry and extended somewhat above the ground; such a structure, commonly known as a mastaba, an outgrowth of the pre-dynastic grave, had a flat surface and sloping sides, a chamber for the ka statue within as well as a shaft leading down to the chamber of the deceased.

Although mummification was almost universal, depending on the means of the family, not all could afford a mastaba; what's more, the lords of the next world, far from being democratic, were respecters of wealth and position.

The pyramid was a further development of the mastaba, its sides continued upward to a point, its area extended, and the burial chamber, if the structure served as a tomb, raised above the ground level. Zoser and Sneferu erected massive mounds of masonry, one terraced, the other left in an unfinished state, and Khufu carried this form to its fullest development in an awe-inspiring monument which is a model of architectural precision and simplicity of line. With its strict adherence to geometric outline, its heavy mass settled solidly in the earth, it looms up on the desert horizon as one creation in man's history capable of defying time and its vicissitudes. Its sides sheathed with polished granite and the sun god's rays bathing its surface, the effect must have been nothing less than startling. Regardless of how it was built or what hidden purpose may underlie its plan, the observer must feel that a man capable of mustering resources for a mass of masonry extending over thirteen and a half acres surely commanded the deepest respect of his subjects. We may say this monument had an astronomical significance more vital to the Egyptian than to us, but surely a simpler device would have served the pharaoh's purpose equally as well; we may conclude it was merely meant to protect the remains of his body and his possessions from the vandal, but it must have been apparent even at that time that the latter could be as resourceful as the architect. Perhaps, from the standpoint of religion, a tomb of such a shape and size would be under the most watchful surveillance of the sun god every hour of the day. We must admit we cannot fully appreciate the Egyptian's passionate thought of converting the ever-changing into the unchangeable.

Pyramids of various sizes continued to be built throughout the Middle Kingdom, but with the coming of the Empire, monarchs and nobles were stowed away in rock-cut tombs in the barren hills near the city of Thebes; mortuary temples, where offerings were presented and services performed, were now put up at some distance from the tomb. The former consisted of a long passageway, often sloping downward, leading through pillared halls and storage chambers to the resting-place of the mummy. These tombs, like that of Tutankhamon, were crowded with armor, furniture, vases, gems, chests, worked out in all the finest materials available, merely to serve the deceased in the next world; what could not be carried into the tomb was painted on the walls with magical intent. Most of the burial places, as secret as their location may have been, were sacked long before the coming of the modern archaeologist.

For architectural purposes the Egyptian was blessed with some of the finest limestone, sandstone, and granite of the ancient world, materials which gave his buildings a solid appearance and made brick only an occasional necessity. The so-called temple of the Sphinx, at the beginning of the causeway leading to Khafre's pyramid, is one of the earliest preserved examples of temple structure. The strict application of the lintel principle in the T-shaped hall, the solid, heavy blocks of stone used in pillar and architrave, and the absence of decorative detail unite to make it a monument of overpowering grandeur. Between the vertical line of the pillar and the horizontal line of the architrave there is no capital to conceal the abruptness of the angle; freestanding pillars are used for the first time;[13] the slits at the top of the walls, to shed light on the interior, may be cited as one of the first known examples of the clerestory. Standing in the center of such a hall lined with towering statues of Khafre himself, the citizen of the Nile must have been duly impressed with the all-powerful divinity that had reduced circumstances to such an uncompromising order, thereby forcing earth and heaven to serve man's needs.

With the passing of the pyramid as a monumental tomb, the same form, reduced considerably in size, was united with the temple, *i.e.*, enclosed within the temple precinct. Among a large number in the late dynasties of the Old Kingdom the sun temple of Nuserre, if we can trust the restoration, had a large platform

---

13. E. B. Smith: *Egyptian Architecture*, New York, 1938, p. 125.

supporting the ritual chambers on three sides; the pyramid rose up awkwardly to the rear of the central space; on each side of the temple was a bark of the sun god. From the Middle Kingdom the temple of Mentuhotep, next to that of Hatshepsut, shows a similar arrangement; here, however, the rooms of the temple were clustered around and behind the pyramid, which must have loomed up as a colossus out of proportion with its surroundings. Eventually the architect saw fit to omit the pyramid from the temple plan.

The pylon temple reached its culmination during the Empire when revenues were pouring in from the provinces to the northeast and from raiding expeditions in the south to help the pharaohs erect large cult and mortuary temples. The usual plan included an avenue approaching the pylon, the loftiest part of the building which resembled two truncated triangles flanking the entrance; before the pylon were monolithic obelisks, generally carved from the granite quarries at Aswan, and flag staves to add a festive appearance. Once inside one found himself in a large, spacious court open to the sky and flanked by columns, the side walls of this court continuing around the whole temple area. The next section was the hypostyle hall, the central aisle raised above the wings on each side to make room for the clerestory; sufficient light was undoubtedly furnished for the high center aisle, but the wings were shrouded in sombre twilight. The sanctuary, the lowest part of the temple, led off from the majestic hall. Openings in the roof afforded a limited amount of light for the priests and pharaoh as they performed the sacred rites on prescribed occasions. Careful planning, dictated by mathematical calculations, astronomical observations and religious scruples, untold labor recruited from the lower classes and war prisoners, a wealth of achievement in sculpture and painting, and an atmosphere of secrecy made this type of building a symbol of Egypt's strength and weakness in the heyday of empire.

The temple at Karnak is the most outstanding representative of the pylon structures. Dedicated to the state divinity Amon-Ra, it was begun already in the twelfth dynasty, rebuilt and added to until the days of the Ptolemies, especially by the more prominent rulers of the Empire. From a distance, this mighty shrine, with its six pylons, must have resembled a sprawling colossus looking out along an avenue of sphinxes to another similar temple at Luxor. In its axis, the walls around the building, the massive architraves and pylons, it heralds the glorification of the straight line. In the great court there must have been a great deal of bustle and noise on the part of visitors and merchants. The common man may have had access to the hypostyle hall where the maze of huge columns, the painting of every available surface, and the semi-darkness filled him with awe. When one realizes that a hundred men could stand on the capital of a column whose diameter is nearly twelve feet, when one gapes at an architrave block weighing nearly one hundred and fifty tons, one is impressed, on the one hand, with the hall's overwhelming size and on the other with the relentless insistence of human desire in imposing its will on stone. Sheer size and a great number of columns filling an interior space may not meet the standards of good architecture, but these and other features have given the structure enough of the sublime to carve a lasting impression on the imagination. The balance of the temple area was taken up with smaller pylons, a festal hall built by Tuthmose III, and ritual chambers.

The main structure, apart from the sacred lake and sub-ordinate buildings, was surrounded by a plain wall which gave the temple a barren appearance from the outside. The interior of the shrine presented a marked contrast to the sunlit walls and the busy life of the court; the silent, half-lit sanctuary, guarding the secrets of ritual, was accessible only to priest and pharaoh. The size of the temple (about 1,200 feet by 360 feet) is made so much the more impressive, like that of the great pyramid, by the predominance of geometric lines and forms; a certain vitality was given here and there by the painting on the columns, by the natural leaves and flowers of the capitals. With all this emphasis on the straight line and symmetry, however, the Egyptian had no scruples about including an appendage like the temple of Rameses III jutting out from the wall of the great court. It lacked, then, the coherence of other temples, a fact we cannot take too seriously when we remember that this building was a national shrine where the national deity guarded the symbols of Egyptian supremacy, where each monarch added a testimony to his own contribution to the glory of empire. Karnak was the focal center of Egyptian national pride, another version of the microcosm corresponding to the macrocosm all around and beyond.

Another temple dedicated to the same divinity and associates at Luxor, while not as overpowering in size, had a touch of elegance and refinement in its "hall of appearances" built by Amenhotep III. The long colonnade in the central section, perhaps originally meant to be the central aisle of a hypostyle hall, left the structure somewhat emaciated in appearance. The most charming of the mortuary temples is unquestionably that of Hatshepsut. Its three terraces, its trees and shrubbery from a foreign clime, the subordination of columns to the prevailing horizontal line, and the lines of the building continuing into the vertical grooves of the cliff created the illusion of a garden growing out of and sheltered by the rock behind it; for all its geometry and pylons it was the most organic of Egypt's larger buildings. Seti I erected an interesting temple, L-shaped in plan, at Abydos, a shrine for seven divinities, especially for Osiris, whose grave was located by tradition on this site; the temple is even better known for its relief sculpture than for its architecture, which is in poor condition today. His son, Rameses II, plundered the works of his predecessors to put up the huge Ramesseum, designed after the palace of the Pharaoh and glorifying his campaign at Kadesh.[14] His rock-cut temple at Abu Simbel is a remarkable product of structural imagination, particularly impressive from the river, but the interior is sadly out of proportion to the colossal statues towering over the observer like subterranean titans. The well-preserved temple of Rameses III at Medinet Habu, in a sense a monument for his victory *terra marique* over the invaders from the north, is a

---

14. E. B. Smith: *op. cit.*, pp. 138-39.

rough imitation of the Ramesseum. Compared to the work of the eighteenth dynasty, later temples are mediocre in workmanship, clumsy in design. Apart from the introduction of the screen wall and a greater variety in capital decoration, the Ptolemies were content to follow established tradition. Our two great losses in Egypt's architecture are the large open-court temple dedicated to the Aton at el 'Amarna and the so-called Labyrinth of the Middle Kingdom, a building devoted to secular as well as religious purposes.[15]

A rigid permanence, again dictated by religious tradition, is the most obvious trait of sculpture on the Nile, suggested partly by the materials in common use, partly by the motives of the figures, and an effort to make the body, even while in motion, subservient to geometric lines. Some of the finest materials—granite, limestone, porphyry, basalt, diorite—were at the sculptor's disposal to help him compete with the decay of time. The free-standing figure, as aggressive as it may seem, is firmly rooted in the floor, its body and appendages conforming to the law of frontality; the relief figure turns the upper part of the body to a three-quarter view to present as much of the body as possible to the observer, the head and legs remaining in profile. To the modern, with his enthusiasm for truth to nature, this spells as much confusion as a Picasso abstraction. Even more puzzling is the fact that these conventions were preserved through centuries, long after the artist had come into contact with the work of the Greek. The laws governing the position of figures and the dominance of the geometric line were already fixed in the pre-dynastic period, then handed down by divine ordinance like ritual procedure. The miracle of Egyptian figures consists in the vivid portrayal of living features within the barriers of an iron-clad conservatism. In their statuary there is so much that is a part of us and so much beyond us!

Where in the history of art can one search for a figure of such sheer strength as the dignitary of the Hesire relief? His assurance borders on arrogance; his purpose is beyond the

---

15. Herodotus, II, 148.

shadow of a doubt; he lives and moves in the prescribed pathway sanctioned by all the authority of the past. He is clothed in all the certainty of the primitive but has achieved a tighter control on his destiny. The village chieftain, despite his more portly figure, maintains the same degree of *hauteur* and at the same time looks out on life with an air of *Gemütlichkeit*; within the framework of authority he can reprove good-naturedly and condone with aloofness; he loves the good life both as it is and as it ought to be. The seated scribe bends before the lord of dictation and flouts his cocksure, bourgeois respectability before the common man; without a full measure of imposed restraint, his pride would degenerate into snobbery. Ra-hotep and Nefert, grafted to thrones of white, looking ahead to a timeless future, take a family pride in having lived the approved life of favored Egyptians; one can only marvel how the sculptor has endowed the pair with an aloof self-satisfaction and avoided tainting them with smugness. These people tell us very plainly and simply that the Egyptian was on a pedestal of natural endowment and achievement, the favorite of the gods living in the best of lands, in time and eternity. They had discovered a rare prescription for welding together the finite and infinite and had enjoyed the present so much more because they knew how to prolong it into the next life.

The portrait of Ra-nefer is another fine example of how the artist could achieve such interesting variety within the limitations of convention. The face is most frank and sincere in expression; the massive shoulders, the chest and arms give the figure its power; the legs and ankles, as in so many others, are clumsy in their modeling. The most awe-inspiring portrait of the Old Kingdom is the statue of Khafre. Seated on a throne which reaches only to the shoulders, the monarch gazes with serene contemplation beyond the here and now. The divinity of the pharaoh is also made obvious by the protecting falcon behind the headdress; the king is both Horus and Osiris, the master of past and future, the channel through which the infinite controls the finite, keeps the sun, moon, and stars in their courses, and causes the Nile to rise and ebb. The face is framed in a geometric pattern formed by the line of the headdress meeting the outstretched wing of the falcon and continuing down along the chest. The upper part of the body, facing straight forward, contrasts its bold modeling with the angular form of the head; the parallel lines of the loin cloth once more follow the shape of the throne, thus emphasizing the arm and hand above. All the lines and contours of this masterpiece have been carefully studied to stress the other-worldliness of the ruler, to show how closely the finite and infinite, this world and the next, are interwoven.

One must be careful not to underrate the ability of this artist because he repeated so much as he worked within the limits of prescribed authority. It is true that he followed definite rules laid down for the proportions of the body.[16] The geometric line, the law of frontality are always in evidence; the lower appendages are for some unknown reason neglected; but in the faces there is a revealing, composite biography. The Egyptian sculptor was convinced that limitations are limiting only for the limited artist.

Reliefs of the Old Kingdom, of which we have a large number from the walls of tombs, were very flat (the figures raised about an eighth of an inch from the background); hence painting was called in to make up for many defects. A certain intimacy reigns in these domestic and agricultural scenes, so different from the austerity of monumental statuary. There are obvious shortcomings in foreshortening and composition, the turning of the head, shoulders, or waist is sometimes awkward, but the introduction of movement and the natural portrayal of animals are testimony to the keen observation of the sculptor. Whenever possible, the human being is rendered in the conventional manner, the eye looking out bird-fashion from the side of the face, both feet, exactly the same, resting flatly on the ground. The man carrying the goat, from Sakkara, is an example

---

16. M. A. Murray (*Egyptian Sculpture,* New York, 1930, pp. 20ff.) gives the canons of proportion and their variations in later periods. Sponenburgh (*Bulletin of the Faculty of Arts of Cairo University* XV, 1953, pp. 83-96) disputes these canons of proportion.

which affords an interesting comparison with the calf-bearer of Greece. In the scenes presenting the throwing of a bull or the fattening of geese we are brought into the home life of the peasant; we can appreciate something of his *joie de vivre*, his love of the natural; we find him considerably far removed from the primitive whose fear of the unknown in his environment prevented him from enjoying everyday experiences.

Within the framework of old conventions, the Middle Kingdom brought with it certain changes, some for the better. The figures of Senusert I and Amenemhet III are seated on the same type of throne. They try to look off beyond the observer with the same impersonal expression, but somehow, whether young or mature, they impress one as youngsters trying to play the roles of their elders in chairs and trappings too large for them. Some portraits, in spite of the bulging eyes, reveal a sad expression. After the period of revolutionary upsets these monarchs were somewhat uneasy beneath the crown; they could no longer feel as secure in their divinity as Khufu and Khafre. The greater emphasis on the human aspect comes out also in the running motifs from the temple of Mentuhetep and the ritual relief of Senusert, a work highly praised for its vigor and motion. The pantomime of the movement, however, is still far removed from the effort necessary to overcome finite limitations; he moves with much the same ease as Mephisto and his horse in Delacroix's lithograph, contrasting with the strained effort of the other horse and rider.[17] It is still a symbolic type of movement, patterned after the subjective interpretation of cosmic motion. In general, the work of this period is more humanly interesting and, therefore, weaker, in general effect, than the work of the Old Kingdom.

The empire brings in its train a cosmopolitanism, a greater insight into the character of the individual, a greater interest in details and accessories which, at first sight, may seem to be an advance but in most cases serve only to detract attention from more careless workmanship. For some unknown reason the eyes are brought too far forward and the ears are frequently too high,

17. R. Escholier: *Delacroix*, Paris, 1926, p. 200.

defects so much more obvious when a head is seen at close range. Pharaohs may be seen in kneeling postures, even prostrate in worship before a divinity, a feature often explained by the influence of Syrian customs. It is true that peoples of the fertile crescent refused to identify the monarch with divinity, but why should Egypt imitate the religious practice of a conquered nation? Akhenaton, the most cosmopolitan in his sympathies, did not succumb to this custom. It seems more reasonable to suppose that the priesthood, which was gaining more and more control of the throne, observed it first and then encouraged it to its own advantage. The desire to show off the pomp and circumstance of empire in the face of foreigners was also reflected in the vanity of fashionable individuals; coiffures, dress, and ornaments called for more attention from the sculptor and painter.

Hatshepsut is a capable but saucy little queen, doing her utmost to justify her position on the throne; Tuthmose III is a conquering soldier, a man of the world and above his world, a ruler of great energy and courage; Amenhotep II is an efficient, somatotonic character, impatient with insubordination; Amenhotep III, the ruler of the golden age, has a somewhat sensuous expression, prefers refinement and moderate luxury; Haremhab is a calculating soldier and statesman. With a little understanding of history, one can see how the sculptor has caught a flash of character in the facial features. They are all cast in the same mold as other rulers, but the mold has become more pliable. They are still willing to conform to the old pattern for the sake of security in that they remain humble servants of Amon until there is no longer an Egypt at their feet. The portrait of Rameses II in Turin has youthful freshness, an alertness, and a spirit of boyish nature which serves as a tonic in a waning period, and the prostrate figure of the same ruler is a fascinating study in line, its balance and rhythm a definite departure from the conventional statue.

Granted the fact that Egyptian sculpture had never been divorced from architectural settings, the colossi of the Empire are hardly an asset to the temple background. How far removed are the pudgy Ramessid giants from the Khafre figures designed for the temple of the Sphinx!

Moreover, the relief figure is carved on walls and pylons without any regard for rules of proportion.[18] The Seti reliefs at Abydos are good reproductions of ritual movement; at first sight the polished surface exaggerates their merit, but closer examination reveals them almost devoid of modeling. Another device to cover up such a defect was the method of cutting figures into the stone, a practice already begun in the Middle Kingdom. The pharaoh, rising up like a fabulous giant, rides roughshod over his diminutive enemies, or holds a number by the hair and smites them with his weapon; only Rameses II achieves genuine drama in a careless composition depicting his struggle at Kadesh. At Medinet Habu both composition and execution are nothing less than sloppy.

The el 'Amarna period, which is not entirely an oasis in Egyptian sculpture, is closely bound up with the viewpoint of Akhenaton, who strove to break away from time-honored conventions. The spirit of an all-pervasive divinity manifests itself in the lushness of vegetation, the flight of birds, the miracles of birth and growth, the intimacy of family communion—all rendered with a greater fidelity to nature, somewhat strange in an Egyptian setting. There is also a tendency to descend from the austere heights of the divine symbol to render objects more alive and conformable to the pulsating surroundings of nature— even the hand extending from the rays of the sun disc. Was this a result of Minoan influence or a reflection of the pharaoh's outlook? Granted the Minoan emphasized a greater fidelity and harmony with nature, he never reproduced the ugly features or abnormalities of the human figure: on one relief Akhenaton appears with a week's growth of beard! The peak of the el 'Amarna achievement is the portrait head of Nefertiti. The line of convention is here strained, while the surface of the head is saturated with a natural sensitivity so much the richer for its binding restraint. The lines defining the features, from the

---

18. E. B. Smith: *op. cit.*, p. 139.

side view or the front, form a clear pattern of rhythmic harmony
covering a dynamic personality like the down of a duckling; it
is the most elegant creation in Egyptian art. From this time
onward the artist is more and more concerned with an effort
to conceal a deterioration of form and modeling by a superficial
prettiness of detail.

In painting the artist had at his disposal lamp black, malachite for green, a blue derived from copper, yellow and brown
from ochre, and white from gypsum. The paint was applied to
a thin layer of gesso, the white of an egg serving as a binding
medium; this method of painting hardly added up to anything
like the fresco of the Minoans. All the way from the remarkable
procession of geese from Medum to the el 'Amarna period we
find the devices of the painter similar to those of the sculptor:
the proportions of the human figure, the perspective, the twist
of the torso, the profile features. On the other hand, the color
brings out an increased emphasis on truth to nature in the faces
of men and women, the feathers of fowl, the fur of the cat,
the green of vegetation, the sparkle of jewelry; the use of
chiaroscuro, in a later period, adds conviction to the running of
animals and the roundness of figures. In every case, however,
the framework of human desire holds within its compass the
uncertain spontaneity of nature and man.

Like his primitive predecessor, the Egyptian found himself
living in a changeable environment, and though this change was
less variable than elsewhere, its unpredictability was still a
dangerous obstacle to his welfare. Uncertainties which threatened him from many sources, especially in the early days of his
culture, called forth awe and fear. In counteracting these dangers,
the early Egyptian had no doubt followed much the same
procedure as most primitives: he had built up a strong subjective
viewpoint; he had sought to make the ever-changing more
regular in various ways; he had dictated to circumstances and
believed in the efficacy of his dictates. In short, he had striven
to subdue finite change by making the pleasing aspects of his
existence as permanent and lasting as possible. It all added up

to a conflict between the infinity of human desire, expressed in so many thoughts and actions, and the caprice of the finite. The Egyptian, however, was different from many ancient peoples in that he never learned to disparage the finite in favor of the negative and so did his utmost to eternalize its agreeable features in concrete, positive terms. Perhaps the germ of such a view lies latent in the efforts of many primitive peoples (which is our main reason for considering the Egyptian after the primitive), but in the civilization of Egypt it is more obvious, especially in the tombs. At any rate, the two realms, the finite and infinite, were so closely interwoven it is difficult to know whether the infinite has been rubber-stamped with the pleasant aspects of the finite or the latter has been permeated with an eternal sameness.

We may say, then, that the other world, or the extension of time into eternity, was like a panoramic and photographic view of the present which the subjective lens had improved and suffused with a transparent, long-range perspective. It was as though one saw the Nile, at one moment, moving from south to north in time and, at the next moment, a photograph of the same Nile through a stereoscope. Perhaps much of this is due to a predominant materialism in the Egyptian's thinking and the ease with which he was able to impress his environment with his conventions. Whatever may have been the reason, such a close identification or assimilation of the two realms had its advantages: one could enter, soon after death, a world already familiar; eternity and infinity were not a denial of the present life; hence there was no reason for practicing asceticism to avoid the temptations of the flesh and the devil; there was no occasion for lofty ecstasy to lift the soul to spiritual heights, no need for the life of reason to ascend to the crystalline sphere of "the divine, and pure, and uniform." [19] There was no contradiction in content between one realm and the other, no paradox of the one and the many, free will and determinism; there was no concern about acquiring original sin by falling from one realm

---

19. Plato: *Phaedo*, 83e.

to the other: one was not wholly good in contrast to the other. Within the security of the infinite the Egyptian could also enjoy a certain amount of humor, which was beyond the reach of some ancient peoples; beyond the fact that it was a smug type of humor, we know very little about its nature.

How did the Egyptian impose regularity and dependability on the caprice of changing events? First, we should examine a number of his early contributions to civilization for the effects of this process. We must also bear in mind that he was the most conservative of ancient peoples, the most resistant to change, and without the impact of the foreign invader, the same practices would have held still more rigid sway throughout his history. One authority assures us that the Hyksos brought in a number of devices and inventions, including the shaduf.[20]

The astronomical observations of the early Egyptian brought forth one of the earliest versions of the solar calendar in which the length of the year was set at three hundred and sixty-five days, by far the best system devised by any of the ancient peoples. Concessions had to be made, of course, to nature; throughout his history time reckonings were made according to three different calendar systems.[21] The night, as measured by the water clock, was divided into twelve hours. In winter, when the nights were long, the hours were correspondingly longer and in summer much shorter. Instead of changing the number of hours from one season to another, the number twelve was scrupulously preserved. Many early peoples have attempted to harness time and the movements of the heavenly bodies to the control of number. And what is number?[22] To us it is a convenient measure of quantity, a counting of what we call units, but to early civilizations it could include what was believed

---

20. H. E. Winlock: *op. cit.*, p. 151. Most authorities would not associate the *shaduf* or loom with the nomadic Hyksos.

21. For a review of the Egyptian calendar and time-reckoning, consult J. H. Breasted, *Time and its Mysteries*, New York, 1936, Series I.

22. L. White (*The Science of Culture*, New York, 1949, p. 292) calls mathematical truths "the product of the mind of the human species." Cf. D. Smeltzer: *Man and Number*, New York, 1958, p. 1f.

to be the essential attributes and character of that which had been counted; it contained what we prefer to call subjective quality as well as objective quantity. In this sense it was a symbol of power used by the subject to control things thus summed up in a number; it consequently made the objective world more certain, regular, and dependable, attributes which charmed the mind of man as late as Pythagoras. I think it can be safely conjectured that much of the knowledge, supposedly secret, of the priesthood in various temples consisted of numbers or numerical symbols highly important in religious ritual. Egyptian mathematics, in general, remained so primitive and stereotyped it made little contribution to the advancement of later science.[23]

Writing, too, was conventionalized at a very early date. One may say that writing is only a convenient method of expression and communication, but in Egypt, where the institutions of early times were sacrosanct, hieroglyphics became the authorized form. Though other forms of writing came into use, the old, approved carvings remained practically the same. Like number they could function as symbols, which, from the religious standpoint, invested with power the object to which they were applied; the agent of magic who knew the secret of the effective use of numbers could apply them to the attainment of his own ends. The writings in the *Book of the Dead* controlled the gods and guardians of the next world, and the pharaoh who knew the secret name of the god held the latter in his power; the cartouche of the ruler summed up all he stood for in the eyes of the populace. Likewise, images, as magical symbols, were stylized and employed as instruments of power by human desire.

Motion involved in change constituted a special problem to one who strove for uniform sameness. The most subjective individual was unable to deny the fact of motion in objective experience, and he knew that a certain amount was necessary in the change of seasons, of day into night if he was to gain a livelihood from the soil. He compromised by standardizing

---

23. O. Neugebauer: *op. cit.*, pp. 72ff.

motion, by making it unvarying and regular and so reduced its
caprice, its frightening uncertainty to a minumum.[24] Such a
motion we find in the running Senusert and above all in the
ritual movements on the walls of the Seti temple at Abydos. At
the Sed festival the pharaoh renewed both his connections with
his ancestors and his power over the people and land of Egypt;
at the festival of Min he was instrumental in renewing the
regenerative powers of the earth. Though we know all too little
about the rituals of these and other festivals, the functions of
the pharaoh on these occasions apparently included movements
symbolic of cosmic and geographical changes necessary to the
material prosperity of all Egypt. The power of the pharaoh
being what it was, he succeeded, by dint of these movements,
in making these changes predictable and regular. Thus the
cosmos was also made to bear the imprint of eternity, thanks to
the power of human desire concentrated in the person of the
king.

Much of all this went hand in hand with magic, or let us
say it was the result of magic prevailing in the subjective viewpoint of so many early peoples. In Egypt, however, the coercion
of the finite into something resembling the infinite was also
manifested in another distinctive way, namely by the static,
geometric line. The outlines of pyramids, temples, and other
buildings were uniformly geometric; the human figure in sculpture and painting minimized the curve and clung to symmetry;
if we may judge from the frequent mention of the number four
in ritual, the land of Egypt was reduced to a four-cornered area
furnished with four posts supporting the canopy of the sky
above. Other peoples used magic as much and more than the
Egyptians and made various attempts to reduce change to
uniformity, but no nation, with the possible exception of the
Chinese, brought about such a subtle interweaving of the finite
with the infinite. It is well nigh incredible that a sculptor could
define a figure with such a static line and concentrate the
qualities of life so vividly in the face! The capitals of columns

---

24. H. Frankfort: *Ancient Egyptian Religion,* New York, 1948, p. 88.

were stylized, but once they were painted, they were as fresh as their prototypes in the marshes! A cat may also obey the law of frontality and at the same time look more catlike than any feline painted by the modern realist. On the plane of practice as well as of thought Egypt was the most self-sufficient land in the history of civilization.

Perhaps it would be well to add here that the Egyptians used the term *ma'at* to designate what we have been trying to describe in a number of paragraphs. This term is sometimes rendered as "order," "right," or "justice," none of which is adequate to include all that is implied in the attempted control, on the part of the subject, of the finite in terms of what we call the infinite.[25] From relief sculpture we also learn that it conjured up in the Egyptian mind, not an abstract concept, but a concrete object with practical implications.

We are now in a position to examine the nature of Egyptian thought. It has already been stated that, for the Egyptian, the distinction between the subjective and objective had little meaning.[26] The two were at hand, however, at the beginning of any thought process without having much significance to him as a conscious thinker. In the light of such a close identification there are a number of differences between Egyptian and the scientific thinking of the modern: first, there was no even balance between the Egyptian subject and object, for the subject was far more important and had a way of dictating to or impressing itself on the object; secondly, as Frankfort tells us, both subject and object were alive; hence the relationship was not that between "I" and "it" but between "I" and "Thou," which in no way alters the uneven balance between the two.[27] The modern can think of himself, if he is not too prejudiced, as an imperfect agent dealing with an inanimate object or another person as

25. J. A. Wilson (*The Burden of Egypt*, Chicago, 1951, pp. 48–49, 119–23) has given the most satisfactory interpretation of *ma'at*.

26. H. Frankfort, *The Intellectual Adventure of Ancient Man*, Chicago, 1946, p. 11.

27. *Ibid.*, p. 4; see also M. Buber: *I and Thou* (trans. by R. G. Smith) Edinburgh, 1952, p. 21.

worthy of consideration as himself, but the Egyptian subject was the more powerful of the two, regardless of how much life and power was in the object; the pharaoh was the master of the god who opposed his coming into the bark of the sun. Thirdly, there was possible, though not necessary, a more complete identification between the subject and object, more than the modern thinker cares to make use of; furthermore, there was a definite integrity and authority attached to human desire which gave no quarter to a qualification based on a possible relationship between two or more objects apart from the subject, and therefore the identification was so much more complete. Such a method of dealing with an object makes the relationship more fixed and self-sufficient until the attention of the subject drifts elsewhere.

Knowledge based on a balanced relationship between the subject and object in scientific thought represents a possibility, or at most a probability, hardly an absolute truth, and this in turn is dependent on other relationships containing still further possibilities; a certain measure of uncertainty threatens both subject and object and their connecting link. What do we mean when we say we know an object? First, we define it by fencing it in with limitations; we single it out as a separate unit to discover its uniqueness, its distinctiveness; we also try to learn what it has in common with other objects and to classify it. We must, then, compare it with other objects, which means establishing new relationships, each one tending to modify the first impression. If we shut out all comparison and concentrate on a single object, how can we learn the unbiased truth about it? If a man knows but one variety of fish, flowers, trees, etc., how can he claim to know much about any of them? From our standpoint, the knowledge of the Egyptian suffered from a lack of comparative values, but he no doubt cherished his own method because of its intensity and what he considered its practical efficacy. It inspired conviction or belief, which is based on the whole truth and nothing but the truth in an absolute sense; uncertainty was beside the point.

The directness and concentration involved in such a view is

due not merely to its personal character but to the subjective nature of human desire; the object, too, as we have said, may be a person without standing a fair chance. In short, it is infinity forcing the finite to take on the stamp of its own mold. Dante's soul is endowed with much the same mode of expression:

> When by sensations of delight or pain,
> That any of our faculties hath seized,
> Entire the soul collects herself, it seems
> She is intent upon that power alone;
> And thus the error is disproved, which holds
> The soul not singly lighted in the breast.[28]

The expression of desire justifies itself. It submits to no compromise and so tends to convert the transient into something more approximate to the unchangeable. Its exclusive concentration accounts for what Frankfort emphasizes as "the various and unrelated approaches" made by the subject to an object which may appear in a different light at different times, depending on the interest of the subject at any particular time.[29] The subject can attach a number of analogies to one or more desirable aspects of an object and shift its attention from one to another without establishing any connection between the objects of attention. The goddess Isis assumes control over a varied number of aspects or functions of nature reflected in the behavior of both man and animal, aspects which seem to us unrelated and inconsistent, because we constantly forget that relatedness is not reality to the Egyptian; the subject, whenever and wherever it turns its attention, sanctifies the object with its own eternal truth.

Sometimes this connection between subject and object is explained in terms of cause and effect, which is very appropriate as long as we know what is meant. Today we are no longer sure we can think of one event exclusively as a cause and another

---

28. *Purgatorio* (Cary's translation) IV; Cf. also my *Two Currents in the Thought Stream of Europe,* Baltimore, 1942, p. 19.

29. H. Frankfort: *The Intellectual Adventure of Ancient Man,* Chicago, 1946, p. 20; also his *Kingship and the Gods,* Chicago, 1948, p. 61.

event as an effect to the same degree. To the emotional person whose life is temporarily ruled by absolutes, such a dictum has been and still is true, but for the scientific thinker they are two events in a pattern of relationships, each of which can be regarded in a certain sense as both a cause and an effect, since each one is open to influences emanating from other events and at the same time influences others as well. In this sense one can no longer think of one as very different from the other. In Egypt, however, where events were not impersonal phenomena but segments of experience teeming with life and personal consequences, where there was but one direct relationship between the seer and the seen, the speaker and the object spoken to, cause and effect assumed a much different character. There the cause was definitely the powerful agent bringing about the effect; it was also the obvious reason for the effect. Like a piston driving into its cylinder, it reached its goal quickly, with undeviating certainty.

Such thinking has nothing in common with our generalities or general laws. We reason by drawing particular inferences from general axioms and call it deductive; or we build up toward a general thesis from particular facts by the inductive method. A general law, like the concept of Socrates, represents a common denominator drawn from particular instances; the general law, then, is dependent on its relationships to particulars and so is incomplete, dangerously subject to revision or rejection in the face of a new set of relationships. The subject of the ancient Egyptian invested the object of its attention with complete uniformity, consistency, conviction, certainty, which gave it far more than we can find in a common denominator. It acquired every advantage with which it could deny the possibility of the exception. The admission of an exterior relationship, of a universal dependent on particulars, in matters of religion, would have spelled defeat. Some simple form of our reasoning, of course, must have been applied by the Egyptian to practical problems without penetrating his consciousness. We may suppose that the formation of symbols for writing, the observation of the heavens, the invention of agricultural implements, the manufacture of jewelry, the process of mummification must have called for more than hit-and-miss trial and error or the unqualified subjective dictation, but this method was ignored when man thought about his connections with divinity and the cosmos. Here the subject reigned supreme; it dispensed revelation which came down perfect from above.

In the light of such thinking it is easier to understand the role played by magic. The subject endowed the letter, the number, the symbol, and the ritual with its own power and used them as tools to gain its ends; it could magnify a finite part into a whole by substituting a man's hair or nail parings for the man himself; it could abbreviate the whole cosmos and deal with it most conveniently and effectively. It was an expedient approach to a world of objects whose interesting attributes had no way of arousing his curiosity unless they happened to answer to the pressing need of the subject, and even then the object counted for little in its own right. With the aid of this type of thinking the magical tool helped to keep the mind, as subjective as it was, in close contact with practice, while our thinking has the advantage of building up theory for scientific development as well as for later application to practice.

How did one man communicate to another what he believed to be a true and certain order of events to engender belief in the other's mind? First, let us state how we try to convince another of the truth of a statement. We summon up one argument after another in support of a thesis, but we know before we begin that all the arguments under the sun cannot approximate absolute truth and may not convince the other party. The Egyptian decked out his thesis in analogies, and since his attention could shift in accordance with his needs, two widely different analogies might stand for the same thing without having too much in common with each other. The bull and ram stood for procreation, the ibis and baboon represented wisdom, simply because one single aspect of these creatures lent suggestive support to the purpose of the subject to the exclusion of a large number of aspects which might contradict his belief, but the Egyptian saw no need for making an embarrassing comparison between two creatures from what we call an objective standpoint. This method still has its place in poetry and art. "A thing of beauty" Keats calls "a joy forever," which makes a good line of poetry; but, to the scientific thinker, it is a nonsensical statement substituting one unknown for another. When Plato found himself at a loss for a convincing argument, he substituted a picture to bridge a gap between two otherwise irreconcilables; these passages make for good reading and may take the place of reasons for the gullible reader without adding much sound support to the point in question. We condemn analogy as comparison based on similarities which frequently turn out to be superficial; for the Egyptian, the single similarity of one feature in the microcosm to another in the macrocosm, regardless of objective incongruities, was magnified to serve as the whole truth. The subjective mind gave it undisputed self-sufficiency and the listener or observer was expected to receive it as such in a moment that had acquired the scope and certainty of the eternal.

Eventually, after the analogy had been used over and over again, the figure was conventionalized into a symbol, a diminutive version of the greater reality. This abbreviated form contained, for the subject with the proper approach, all the substance and value of its greater counterpart and made it so much easier for man in his capacity of magician to deal with the world at large. All such symbols as the crook, the flail, the ankh and those which passed into hieroglyphics were invested with uncompromising power by the subject to keep the cosmos moving in a pathway of regularity. And because the cosmos is a moving entity, it occurred to the subject at an early date that, by moving the symbols in a desired pattern and by moving along with them, the motions of the world could be controlled effectively. This is the pattern of thought behind religious ritual. At certain definite times of the year a ritual was enacted by a powerful subject or magician to further such motions of the cosmos, manifest in the change of seasons, and make them comply with the practical needs of the people. The great ritual celebrated at Abydos involved the symbolic movements of

Osiris as lord of the Nile, their effect on Isis, the power of fertility of the soil, and counteracted the opposition of Set, the ruler of the desert. So much of the movement of sculpture and painting is symbolic and ritualistic in character, so much of it has been eternalized by the infinite power of subjective desire! The power of the spoken word in the actual performance supplemented the action of the ritual, both imitative in character. In this dual expression the performance exerted a two-fold power over the cosmos and the stress laid on the analogy impressed both the eyes and ears of the audience.

The pharaoh assumed a preponderant role in Egyptian life because he was the great subject dealing with the phenomena of the cosmos as inferior objects and because he was most capable of keeping it in motion for the best interests of the people; he was largely responsible for maintaining a close connection between the finite and infinite. How was it possible for one man to become such a power in a nation's affairs? He was not only a man, he was a divinity; he was not only ruler of the land of the Nile, he was endowed with the greatest power, subjectively speaking, in the world of gods and men. As we have already seen, divinities could suffer harm; hence they could not be called omnipotent in a strict sense of the term, but the pharaoh was Horus in this life and Osiris in the next world. When the Egyptian called him Osiris, he meant that when the ruler passed from this life, he joined his ancestors, who had been rulers in their mortal incarnations, forebears who still reigned in power in another world of the infinite. As Horus he was another manifestation of the same power entering on its career of a ruling pharaoh in the finite present. The connection between the past, the present, and the future was continuous, which means the power of this ruler was eternal. It was like an infinite sequence of power which became manifest in the finite only during the mortal life of the ruler. He was Osiris when one looked back to his connections with his ancestors;

---

30. Cf. H. Frankfort: *Kingship and the Gods,* Chicago, 1948, p. 47.

he was Horus when one looked ahead. As the great subject he was the central figure in rituals which prevented the motions of the cosmos from being chaotic;[30] he was a *sine qua non* to the welfare of every Egyptian. It was incumbent on him to renew his powerful connections with cosmic forces in an annual festival, an act one may regard as magic on a large scale. In the light of such functions one can understand why the Egyptian was in such a state of despair between the Old and Middle Kingdoms when the ruler was tottering on his throne. Not only was his temporal security at stake but also the indispensable connection between Egypt and the eternal order of things, for once this was broken the Egyptian was exposed to gods who were not by nature good and merciful but capricious in their behavior toward men. This connection also explains why the populace as a whole never rebelled against the power of their king, since the theory of government, like that of any magic, was as right as god and man could make it, regardless of any shortcomings cropping up in practice.

This connection between king and people being so vital, it imposed certain duties on both parties and made the monarch an absolute ruler in religion and government. Europeans are inclined to think of the pharaoh as Rousseau thought of the French monarch, as an arch oppressor, driving his people on to build pyramids and tombs, taxing them to the limit and maltreating them in every possible way, whereas this type of government was based on a most binding contract for the mutual benefit of both parties. We must grant that under every absolute form of government there is a single one or a small minority which issues orders and a large majority obeys without too much open objection; unless there is a large number ready to accept and obey, the ruler cannot long remain in power. The government of Egypt, however, was not a tyranny in our sense of the term, even if it was far removed from a democracy. The pharaoh accepted his destiny and its responsibilities just as the people accepted their position. Did a pharaoh ever decide the routine of his existence was unendurable and then abdicate?

And how would the people have dealt with such a monarch? He would no doubt have met with the same fate as the early magician suffering a loss of subjective power, and the pharaoh was a more exalted successor of the primitive magician. Both parties, the ruler and the governed, were cooperating to keep the cosmos running in good order, and since there was only one course it could take to benefit all Egypt and because the pharaoh had the power to keep it in that course, why should there be any superfluous questions? Freedom of thought on the larger issues of life was an invitation to mutual destruction.

It follows, then, that government had to be supported by religion, for religion, after all, was concerned not merely with the soul's welfare but also for man's material welfare in this world and the next. The Egyptian, because the infinite was so closely bound up with the finite, saw no reason for separating the spiritual from the practical, for relegating the one to religion and keeping the other under the control of secular government. This would have broken up the unity of his life and defeated the whole program of the subjective viewpoint. Both aspects were united under the central authority of the pharaoh, who was both man and god and who, therefore, was never bothered with the objections of a dissenting voice to the exercise of absolute power. Since it was possible to keep the cosmos in order by the pharaoh's divine ordinance (the Egyptians believed it had been effective in practice for centuries) there was no reason why it should not work in government. The Egyptian was not comparative enough in his thinking to realize that his conclusion about the cosmos was an afterthought identified with an order already established by nature, while its successful application to government required practical demonstration. Subjective desire is perfect, uncompromising, and arbitrary; it has no respect for a distinction between *ante hoc* and *post hoc*. Naturally, perfect orders issued by a perfect dictator did not meet with perfect fulfillment in the finite. Here, as in the case of the failure of magical intent, the principle was not questioned and therefore the infallibility of divinity remained unsullied. This accounts

largely for the fact that the identity of religion and government
and the form of government itself were never exposed to doubt
by the Egyptian.

Knowledge, as we have said, was tantamount to revelation,
coming out of the infinite without any apology or qualification,
an ultimatum from the subject to the object. We say the
acquisition of knowledge breeds new problems and question
marks in the mind, whereas the stupid person sometimes glories
in the security of his ignorance. What is a problem? A problem
implies a difference between what the subject wants and what
it may have from a given object, and when both are finite in
character, some adjustment on the part of the subject is necessary. New question marks come up because of other relationships
arising in the larger pattern of which both or either the subject
or object may be a part. But if the source of knowledge is in the
infinite, knowledge itself must be perfect; furthermore, if the
connection between a powerful subject and an object is direct
and exclusive of all relationship, why should there be any
problems or questions? The object, however insignificant, was a
passive recipient in the Egyptian's field of attention, it served
as a mirror in which subjective exclusiveness reflected its perfection. If the Egyptian was told by divine authority that the
waters of the Nile would rise at a certain time, he believed
what he was told. The modern would say it was a foregone
conclusion in the mind of the peasant who had seen the same
thing happen at the same time in previous years. But this is
not at all the case. Without the subjective power of the pharaoh
brought to bear on the movements of nature in terms of ritual,
the peasant could never be sure of any seasonal recurrence.

Of morality in our sense of the term we find very little among
Egyptians. A moral person requires a center of moral responsibility lodged within himself, a force strong enough to induce
a man not only to choose between right and wrong but to
carry out his choice in practice. In a program which grants the
subject unlimited power over an object, in accordance with the
methods of magic, there is no opportunity for the development
of self-responsibility or the freedom to choose between right

and wrong; almost anything was possible as long as one possessed the proper formula to gain an end. The direct command of the pharaoh was so cogent that a law code was apparently unnecessary to act as a restraint on human behavior. Whether we listen to the warning of a ruler to his son, to the admonitions passed on the student or to the advice of Ptahhotep, the rule to be observed was expediency rather than moral precept. To avoid the wrath and punishment of a man superior in rank, it was a matter of discretion to obey, but once the eye of authority was absent, there was no guarantee of good behavior; the more numerous the officials, the more likelihood there was of corruption. If the gods, who were not good by nature, were not moral in their dealings with one another, why should man be otherwise? Much of the magic in the *Book of the Dead* was an asset in concealing the wrongs the Egyptian had committed in this life. It follows, then, that fear, as ineffective as we know it to be, was the most ominous threat authority could hold over the head of a citizen. When the power of authority was removed, the ruler's magic was weakened, his curses were of no avail, his tomb could be plundered; one pharaoh might even commit sacrilege on another. In a land where human desire and geography conspired to make the ruler such a centralized authority, one who could "hold infinity in the palm" of his hand and "eternity in an hour" twenty-four hours a day, where man and his universe were fitted together in such a binding system of magic, moral responsibility had little chance to survive. Where every subject was privileged to use anyone or anything as a means to an end, there could be no mutual feeling of trust between one man and another.

The artist was also pressed into the service of magic to such an extent it is difficult to know how the plastic arts would have survived apart from the ritual and the tomb. Egyptian art, like many a subjective tool, may be thought of as a summary treatment of the macrocosm, a projection of human desire to deal arbitrarily with certain otherwise stubborn problems of life. There may have been some feeling for decorative qualities and monumental massiveness, but so far as we know, the Egyptian was little concerned about aesthetics. Perhaps the average citizen may have admired walls covered with painted reliefs, but surely their primary purpose was to eternalize the pleasant features of this life, and because art never achieved emancipation from the subjective viewpoint, the artist never acquired an independent personality. If art, however, is a form of self-identification, the Egyptian found it by reproducing the concrete blessings of his good earth and bounteous Nile.

The Egyptian made little or no contribution to the democratic viewpoint because the all too human desire for security met with fewer obstacles, with the possible exception of China, than elsewhere in the ancient world. The primitive magician was in control of perfect connections between the causes issuing from the microcosm to unerring effects in the world at large, and the pharaoh, by virtue of his control over the cosmos, was in a position to play the role of divine magician in religion and government. Theoretically there could be no mistake or tragedy; not that the subject never missed the mark, but a perfect sequence between cause and effect, in a subjective viewpoint, could afford to give no quarter to the exception; for the same reason there was no way of improving on such a sequence; it was beyond qualification and hence perfectly sterile. For the imperfection of the finite the lord of the two lands showed only a "wrinkled lip and sneer of cold command."

THE MESOPOTAMIAN

WHILE MESOPOTAMIA, or the land between the two rivers, was, under favorable conditions, one of the most fertile regions on the earth's surface, it was by no means a ready-made paradise for man. The ancient Sumerians, along with their successors, were made to realize, like Faust, that life in the face of so many obstacles is a matter of constant striving to achieve some sort of victory over circumstances. In the first place, it was a land that had to be irrigated, if crops were to flourish in the long dry season of the summer. The climate was very capricious in its behavior; blasts of wind and rain would swoop down from the higher areas, leaving death and destruction in their wake and making control of the flood waters more difficult than in Egypt. The warm and muggy air of summer made the labor on the canals and in the fields so much the more burdensome. Because of the storms, canals had to be kept in repair year after year to prevent the land from lapsing back into sterile aridity, a task which no doubt occupied a number of laborers during much of the year; leisure must have been a rarity for the lower classes. Moreover, all buildings had to be constructed of baked or sun-dried bricks drawn from the rich clay deposits along the banks of the rivers. All this—cultivating crops, repairing canals, building walls and temples, contributing to religious worship and sacrifice, and defending the land from invaders —must have made the Mesopotamian the busiest toiler of the ancient world.

When we speak of Mesopotamia we refer to all the region between the Tigris and Euphrates, including the Assyrian plateau to the north and the adjacent areas along the riverbanks. The two rivers, flowing in a general direction from northwest to southeast into the Persian Gulf, were almost as vital to the welfare of the people as the Nile to the Egyptian but not by any means as well behaved. In the spring when they overflowed their banks, the silt was left as a rich deposit, and throughout the season water was carried by a network of canals through all the land of lower Mesopotamia. In the course of the intervening centuries the growing deposits at their deltas have extended the land for more than a hundred miles into the gulf, the two rivers now issuing from one mouth, whereas in ancient times there was probably an extensive area of swampland stretching some distance above the old shoreline; the city of Eridu, now far from the sea, was much nearer to the coastline in the days of the Sumerians. The whole region of southern Mesopotamia, which at one time extended eighty miles from one river to the other, is now comparatively desolate, dotted with mounds left by ancient settlements, because the physical geography of the region has changed and irrigation is no longer customary. To the west of the Euphrates and east of the Tigris there lay a desert wasteland whence newcomers and marauding parties might invade the prosperous cities that had to rely largely on walls for defense. In the distant north and at some distance to the east in Elam the mountains afforded a refuge for barbarous, nomadic tribes.

In a country which boasted little if any natural defense, the outsider, looking for a place to settle in the sun, could fall upon the Sumerian with little notice and cause untold damage; there was nothing of the security enjoyed by the Egyptian. What is more, since the land had few natural resources such as good stone and metal, these products had to be imported from a distance for the artisan who fashioned them into implements and wares, which in turn were used as articles for export. Silver was rare, gold and tin were almost unknown except as foreign imports, and good stone from the north was too expensive to be used for building purposes. But there were compensations in the geographical position: Babylon lay on the crossroads for all the trade passing from the Far East through the fertile crescent into Syria and Egypt as well as Asia Minor and the Danube region.

Such a center of trade developed a thriving merchant class that no other ancient land could boast of. Moreover, the soil was so fertile its yield of barley and wheat, as we learn from Herodotus, was unexcelled.[1] Cattle, which were pastured on the grasslands of the northern plateau, furnished meat and leather for articles of export. Rich clay deposits along the rivers provided material for pottery, tablets for writing, and bricks for walls and buildings. The palm was the most prolific among trees. There were plenty of fruits and vegetables; there was wool for the textile industry. With the development of trade and business there came wealth and money to build the cities with their better homes, their palaces and temples, the ziggurats and fortification walls. Trade also encouraged a greater diffusion of culture throughout the Near East, which helps to explain why this people's influence was extended farther than that of Egypt and why cuneiform became the *lingua franca* of merchants and diplomats.

The Sumerians, the earliest known people to settle north of the Persian Gulf, came from some uncertain locale in the north some time after the close of the neolithic period. How far advanced they were at the time cannot be determined, but most authorities agree they did not belong to the Semitic groups. Short and stocky, they set to work at draining the marshes, tilling the soil, and digging canals for irrigation; on higher terrains they pastured their cattle, sheep, and donkeys. First they built their homes of mud and straw; later the more wealthy used brick to construct more solid and spacious dwellings, all grouped around the temenos, which included the ziggurat, the temple of their god, and the palace of the ruler. The temenos was the matrix of the whole city. In addition to the dwelling of the ruler, who was at the same time the chief priest of the god, it afforded a home for the priests and priestesses in charge of the temple, the busy center of secular and religious life. The cities which dotted the plain frequently quarreled over property and water rights, resulting in wars fought out by the rulers as well as the patron divinities of the cities who, it was claimed, led their respective

---

1. I, 193.

armies into battle, who mourned with the city in defeat and rejoiced with the victorious host. On Sumerian reliefs we see the soldiers marching in a compact formation, armed with shields, helmets, and spears, and in later times, accompanied by chariots. The defeated city might be destroyed and its population enslaved, or it might receive a governor appointed by the victorious commander. In times of peace a surplus in produce and manufacture found an outlet in trade with more distant peoples, who in turn sent their merchants into Mesopotamian markets. Later a desire to control the source of raw materials and trade routes encouraged wars on a larger scale, all of which made a city like Babylon a thriving center of exchange, a Mecca for the caravan, a busy market teeming with exotic merchandise and confusing tongues.

The government of the city was in charge of the ensi, as they called him, who functioned as the representative of the city's patron divinity, the highest civil authority, and the final court of appeals. Since he was the chief priest, he ruled by divine right and his authority was absolute; although he was not a divinity incarnate like the pharaoh, his office was sanctioned by divine approval, and for all practical purposes he exercised the same prerogative, except in the presence of the gods, where he was much more humble. Once every year, during the city's chief festival, the contract between divinity and ruler was renewed to insure some measure of security for the people during the forthcoming year. In wartime he was commander-in-chief of the army, marching out to the attack or defending the city at the head of his troops, and no doubt he suffered the greatest disgrace and punishment in case of defeat. In peacetime he was in charge of any new undertaking or building enterprise, unhampered save by revelation coming from some form of divination, but his special boast, according to the inscriptions, was the canals he kept in good condition, a fundamental requirement for economic prosperity. It was also his business to formulate laws, to draw up regulations for trade, to watch over the standards for weights and measures, and to keep the calendar in order. Finally, he was in charge of walls, temples, and public buildings.

Among all the cultural achievements of this people initiated before the third millennium, their writing stands in first place. The story of its evolution is an interesting one.[2] From the copious samples we possess we learn the first phase was characterized by pictographs or drawn pictures to indicate to the reader the objects the writer had in mind; this method was convenient at the time for practical purposes but awkward for recording abstractions and verbs. The next step was the ideograph, a single picture like the barking dog before a house in Pompeii or a composite picture like the signs of the zodiac to convey a message on a higher mental plane. Then some ingenious scribe invented the use of signs to express sounds and so created phonetic writing, which means the hand had only to follow the articulations of the voice to make the meaning more unequivocal. The first material for writing may have been wood, which eventually gave way to clay because the latter, being a softer medium, required only an impression, while wood demanded carving. In the hand the writer held a reed stylus with a triangular point for making wedge-shaped impressions on the moist clay, whence the term cuneiform is derived. An instrument of this kind limited the scribe to certain shapes or patterns and tended to stylize the signs to the point where the original pictograph could no longer be recognized, but at the same time the clear-cut signs made for pronounced clarity, compactness, and facility in making records. Crystallization, however, did not set in until an efficient form of writing had been developed, one useful for all practical purposes of the Sumerian, the Babylonian, and the Assyrian.

This type of writing was used for recording laws, for historical documents, for all business contracts and commercial transactions. We find it on reliefs running like a transparent screen across the lower half of the field of illustration, on stone steles, and, above all, on countless clay tablets. Such tablets made up the library of Assurbanipal. Every transaction in a Sumerian city required a written document and, although the general run

---

2. For an interesting discussion of cuneiform consult E. Chiera: *They Wrote on Clay*, Chicago, 1938, pp. 50ff.

of the people was unable to write and few could read, there was always a scribe at hand with a supply of moist clay at every temple and market. The contract was recorded on a tablet and enclosed within an envelope, also of clay, and a copy of the same contract was written on the outer surface. The record within could not be tampered with, except by breaking the clay envelope. Furthermore, every agreement after 2000 B.C. had to be signed by both parties plus the witnesses, and because few could sign their names, the cylinder seal came into common use; these seals, carried around the neck, impressed the tablet with scenes usually drawn from religion and mythology. The contract was inviolable, for once the inner tablet had hardened it was out of the question to cover it with a new envelope because the outer covering of moist clay, covering a tablet already hardened, would crack in the process of drying and contracting; the agreement was more secure against forgery than any safeguard of the modern banker.

The calendar of the Mesopotamian, which was lunar instead of solar in its divisions, was more cumbersome for this very reason but still merits attention because of its later adoption by the Greeks. The moon, attached to a male divinity, was evidently more important than the sun to a nation of star-gazers who believed its rotating shadow, directed toward the earth, had some bearing on the fertility of the soil; the moon's position among the stars was also significant in revealing the will of the gods. The year, then, was divided into twelve months of thirty days each, making a year of 360 days, which required an occasional intercalary month called the second Adar. Before the time of Hammurabi each one of the city states had its own calendar, the ensi making an addition whenever he deemed it necessary to meet the demands of the sun's course. In spite of its cumbersome character, the Sumerians clung to their lunar calendar and went on to make it more exact, which also means they made it more complicated. For marking time they used the sun-dial and the water clock. The later Babylonians also measured the periodicity of eclipses and may have been familiar with the precession of the equinoxes. The planets and many of the fixed stars were studied by their observers, not so much for scientific purposes as for astrology, a form of magic which probably produced the signs of the zodiac. Although they made use of the decimal system in their mathematics, the sexagesimal system, undoubtedly influenced by the lunar calendar, was more popular. They had no sign for zero, but the fact that they left an empty space for it points to an awareness of its significance.[3]

The principal cities of Sumeria included Eridu, the nearest to the sea in early times; Ur, the seat of worship of the moon-god and the traditional home of Abraham, Larsa, Lagash, Erech, Umma, and Shuruppak. Somewhat to the northwest and following the two rivers upstream lay the territory of Akkad, already settled by Semites when we first hear about it. Their most flourishing city at this time was Kish. About the middle of the third millennium these Semites, who were capable organizers and administrators but otherwise dependent on the culture of Sumeria, produced an able man in the ruler Sargon, reputedly of lowly origin, who united the whole region of southern Mesopotamia into a single federated kingdom. This brought to an end the political power of the native ensis as well as the internecine wars between the cities. By means of an efficient military machine he extended his conquests through the upper fertile crescent to the Mediterranean to insure the control of certain economic resources needed at home. Naram-Sin, an aggressive successor, held the empire intact by waging a number of wars with rebels and border peoples—a tall, slender but vigorous warrior, as a sculptured relief reveals, torturing his enemies in true Mesopotamian fashion. After invasions by the Amorites and Gutians from the north had broken up the Akkadian power, the Sumerian cities once more asserted themselves under men like Gudea of Lagash and Ur-Nammu of Ur. Soon after the beginning of the second millennium the Semites under Hammurabi, one of the most capable rulers of Babylon, again united the Mesopotamians into a well-organized empire.

Hammurabi was both a capable strategist and a good

3. Cf. O. Neugebauer: *The Exact Sciences in Antiquity,* Princeton, 1952, p. 16.

administrator, one who saw to it that his people were protected from the inroads of enemies and improved the condition of the land itself, magnified the city of Babylon into the leading center of the country, and formulated an efficient law code. Recent discoveries tell us that his code, while it is the most complete example we possess, was based on earlier laws drawn up by the Sumerian cities. In general, one may say the code reflects the viewpoint of a very practical people who knew how much man's welfare depended on right action within the community, a code which also served well for the merchants, always property conscious and insisting on fair play in contracts. Other modern features include the marriage laws, those dealing with inheritance, the emphasis on the rights of women, all pointing to a highly developed social consciousness. The preference granted to the aristocrat is, of course, to be expected, but the application of the *lex talionis* may seem out of keeping with the otherwise fair regulations of the code, if we forget that fear was also, here in Mesopotamia, considered the most effective road to obedience. The judge, we may be sure, was no more inclined to be lenient than the average general presiding over a court-martial. Today the medical practitioner would hesitate to resort to surgery if he knew a failure might entail the loss of one of his limbs, and contractors would be few and far between, if they faced the prospect of losing a son because one of their constructions had caused the death of the owner's son, but we must recall that life was very precarious in Mesopotamia; disaster, in one form or another, was constantly flirting with man. We must admit, too, that the principle of laying the burden of proof on the accuser was known, but what was the nature of the proof? A man, we learn, could divorce his wife for being wasteful, but what was the proof in this case and how was its validity established? [4] In spite of our ignorance of their court procedure the code stands out as the most distinctive and progressive contribution of a viewpoint quite different from that of the Egyptian.

About the middle of the eighteenth century B.C. a large group

---

4. For a review of the code of Hammurabi consult P. Carlton: *Buried Empires*, New York, 1939, pp. 253-263.

of Indo-European people, the Kassites, invaded lower Mesopotamia and established themselves as rulers in Babylon. The advantage they enjoyed, from a military standpoint, over the natives lay in their use of cavalry, the horse being comparatively unknown between the rivers up to that time. There is hardly a mention of raids or war, which may mean their invasion was largely a matter of gradual infiltration. Although, in one respect, they might be called cultural parasites who made little or no contribution to the civilization they found, we must credit them with good sense for allowing the common people to go their customary way in trading, in practicing the arts and crafts, in social customs and religious worship.

In the meantime the Assyrians in the north, hemmed in by the Mitanians and the Hittites, were growing slowly and surely. Once these two enemies were disposed of by incursions surely. Once these two enemies were disposed of by incursions from Egypt and the northwest, the Assyrians invaded Babylon about 1250 B.C. Mesopotamia changed masters once more, but again there was no occasion for a cultural upset, for these Assyrians, whose chief cities Ashur, Calah, and Nineveh were on the upper reaches of the Tigris, had already adopted the writing, the calendar, and much of the religious tradition and other cultural assets of the south. The history of Assyria, prior to 900 B.C. was largely a matter of military exploits to render boundaries secure and to put down rebellions. After that date much the same procedure was followed to safeguard what security they had attained, but since the scale of operations was more extensive and Babylon was included in their empire, their activities became more significant. Ashurnazirpal and Tiglath-Pilezer brought the military machine of the Assyrians to its peak of efficacy by the use of siege engines, by novel devices in cruelty, and by transferring certain factious elements in the provinces to a completely different locale. Sargon II warred constantly through the whole valley and the fertile crescent against Elamites, Medes, Phrygians, Syrians; he also had time to build a most impressive palace for his capital at Khorsabad. Sennacherib, aside from the usual conquests of an Assyrian king, is known for his impatience with Babylon, the most favored and fickle of Assyrian subjects. Like Poland in modern European diplomacy, Babylon, in spite of her cultural prestige, was an eyesore in Assyrian administration and, after repeated attempts to keep her peacefully within the fold, Sennacherib leveled the city to the ground and slew the inhabitants. Esarhaddon, repentant for his father's hasty harshness, rebuilt the city and its shrines; he also added Egypt as a province to his empire. Ashurbanipal, judging from the art of the period and the tablets of his library, lived out the Indian summer of Assyrian glory, for soon after his death enemies of long standing crowded in on Nineveh and destroyed it so completely that Xenephon, passing it on his famous march to the sea, was unable to identify the site.

The land of Assyria was a broad plateau without any natural barriers to serve as defenses, a fact which contributed to the development of a strong military power. Buffeted about by peoples around them in their early history it was only natural for them to grow impatient with recurring invasions until they fought back and eventually acquired the reputation of being the most warlike and cruel of ancient peoples. And despite any attempt to apologize for them, they were cruel beyond a doubt.[5] Ashurnazirpal boasts of having burned some of his captives, of cutting off ears, fingers, and tongues, and binding heads to posts. For offensive weapons they had the bow, the spear, and the chariot; their cavalry was of the best; no city was proof against the battering ram they brought into the field. They knew too that the best type of defense was an offensive attack; in fact they very seldom found themselves on the defense. Their expeditions, for the most part, took on the form of plundering or punitive raids and so accomplished little for the organization or improvement of the empire. Once a rebellious city had been leveled to the ground, its people torturously slain or maimed, its crop of grain ruined, its cattle driven off for booty, they felt the rebels should have learned a lesson. All in vain! The Assyrians, we conclude, should also have profited from the experience

---

5. A. T. Olmstead: *History of Assyria,* New York, 1923, pp. 645ff.

of repeated rebellions, but evidently the same procedure was
followed from one reign to another. We also get the impression
that, as long as natives were available for the army, they gloried
in their military prowess; never do we hear of a monarch weary
of war. They loved action; they loved an overt display of power,
and when the monarch was not on the warpath, he was building
a mighty palace or hunting the wild beast. They were, of course,
interested in agriculture and herds of cattle, but they neglected
trade. As soon as their armies had exhausted the native population, their economy failed and the vengeance they had been
storing up for centuries in subject peoples brought about
complete annihilation in 612 B.C.

What began as a means to an end—the emphasis on military
power—and later became almost an end in itself exhausted the
resources of Assyria, so that once she was brought to her knees
there was no hope of a comeback. Babylon, however, was on
her way to a revival despite the number of upsets and destruc-
tions she had suffered at the hands of various enemies, because
she had resources other than military. The Chaldaeans, a people
that had never been conquered by the Assyrians, took over the
leadership of Mesopotamia and made Babylon once more the
queen city of the east soon after the fall of Nineveh. After
Babylon had joined hands with the Medes, she continued where
she had left off before the rise of Assyria. Nebuchadnezzar, the
king the Hebrews condemned to eat grass, soon consolidated
Babylon's position and made her a thriving city of traders,
manufacturers, and builders. On the surface, he seems to have
followed the Assyrians in the ruthlessness of his campaigns, in
uprooting rebellious peoples and was evidently successful enough
to achieve some years of peace for the enhancement of his
capital city. In the west he played the usual role of an eastern
conqueror by putting Egypt in her place, overthrowing Judah,
all but capturing Tyre, and carrying the Jews into the "Babylonian Captivity," but at home he was responsible for a new Babylon
with its strong walls, its wide processional street running the
full length of the city, its "Tower of Babel," its gate of Ishtar,
and the hanging gardens built for his Median queen. While

Nabonidus, one of his successors, was delving into the archae-
ology of religion and quarrelling with his priests, Cyrus had
united the Medes and Persians under his leadership. In 539 B.C.,
because of dissensions in the government of Babylon, the Persian conqueror easily took over the city and made an end of the
political power of Mesopotamia.

The Mesopotamian pantheon, made up of divinities originally associated with natural phenomena, maintained that
association for the most part, even after theology had made
changes to suit political conditions or partially abstracted the
divinities from their early domains. Although they were supposedly born in the same era and enjoyed family connections
with each other, there was nothing like the family nucleus one
finds on Mount Olympus; in this respect they were similar to the
gods of Egypt, but they differed from the latter in being less
static and by expressing themselves, like their worshippers, in
ruthless physical action. They revealed no bond of sympathy
in their interests beyond a cooperation in emergency out of pure
expediency and a mutual agreement to keep man in his place in
the mortal sphere. Capricious to the extreme, they acted without
any reasonable motive, leaving man powerless to fathom the
purpose of their designs. Men, instead of being children of the
gods, were mere slaves created to till the soil, to build their
temples, offer sacrifices around which the gods crowded "like
flies" for their own satisfaction. Because of this absence of a
moral feeling between man and his god, there was a mutual
distrust which prompted man to employ magic to pry into the
secret intent of divinity, to enjoy a small measure of good
fortune by stealing a march on his taskmasters. He would pray
and praise without being at all sure the gods were paying any
attention; first he feared and then tried to please to the best of
his knowledge.

In the center of the earth, which, according to their cosmology, was an inverted boat like that the Sumerians used in river
transport, was the high mountain of Enlil and on the eastern
and western extremities the mountains of the sunrise and sun-

set.[6] Water, in turn, circled around the outside rim of the earth and filled the cavity beneath it. There was also water in the heavens above to account for rainfall. The underworld, the inevitable rendezvous of the dead, was a cavernous hollow beneath the surface of the earth, removed from the light of the sun and the power of the gods of the upper regions, and the sky above was a hemispherical bowl placed over the earth, supported by four posts embedded in the water beyond the limits of dry land. The sun rose up through an eastern gateway and passed through another in the west before it disappeared, returning to the east along a course outside the bowl of the sky. The moon, when invisible to man, likewise hid behind the dome of the sky, but the stars had their assigned places within the bowl. Here as elsewhere in Sumerian religion the numbers three, four, and seven played a role in the divisions of heaven, earth, and the world below, in most cases an arbitrary interpretation to make the universe conform to a subjective, numerical pattern. The composition of the universe at the beginning of things passed under the title of Apsu, analogous to chaos or a formless state of things. As in the cosmology of the Greeks, the Sumerians could conceive neither of a time when there was nothing nor of a god who created something out of nothing. Next we hear of a conflict between divinities, probably descendents of Apsu, who championed order in the universe, and a group of monstrous beings headed by Tiamat, the wife of Apsu and the mother of the gods. This conflict, the most violent before the creation of man, ended with a victory for the gods intent on converting chaos into some kind of order, an order which man, a later creation, was expected to support. What was meant by order? Undoubtedly the "disposition of things," as they called it, referred to divisions and limitations imposed on the primeval chaos, the assignment of certain sections and functions of the universe to definite divinities. The term apparently had only cosmic significance; since man had not yet come on the scene, it certainly had nothing of the far-reaching implications of the Egyptian ma'at.

6. Cf. Diodorus, II, 31, 7; also Herodotus I, 194.

The Sumerian pantheon was headed by Anu, whose province was the sky and who was often referred to as the father of the gods. In divine affairs his advice was often sought; when one divinity stepped beyond his bounds, complaints were registered with Anu; when the gods met in council, he presided. He was, however, too far beyond the reach of man, too cosmic in character, to be vitally concerned with the interests of mankind, and so, like Uranus, Varuna, and Odin, he was gradually relegated to an impersonal background. His main shrine was located at Uruk. Ea, whose chief shrine was in Eridu on the Persian Gulf, was the god of water and the one divinity who, from the time of man's creation, had his interests at heart more than the other gods; yet he was careful, as we observe in the story of Adapa, not to allow man to achieve immortality. His attachment to man probably stems from the fact that water was of prime importance in the life of the people; moreover, it was a primary element in the universe, several of the divinities having been identified with this element before they rose to other realms. It was Ea who had come out of the water to teach men how to write and count, to build their cities and dig their canals as well as to till their fields. His priests can be identified by the scaly garments they wore during rituals. Whether it was the cause or result of Ea's connection with man's cultural progress, water somehow became associated with wisdom, and the god of water became a patron of knowledge and learning, much of which was so ancient man had forgotten how he acquired it and so ascribed it to revelation. Enlil, the most ruthless god of the pantheon, who dwelt on the great mountain of the earth and whose temple was known as the mountain house, was the ruler of the storm cloud. It was he who brought so much misfortune to man, who once had sought to destroy him in a flood, and who, in the early version of the creation story, destroyed Tiamat and her cohorts to bring about the established order of things. This god, whom the Semites called Bel, had his chief seat of worship at Nippur. The three male divinities, Anu, Ea, and Enlil were often grouped together and known as the great trinity.

Among the Sumerians the day began at sunset because the

moon god, Sin, was of much greater importance than among other early peoples. The reasons for his importance are largely conjectural: one may say this heavenly body can be seen more clearly in relation to the stars and planets than the sun by day; it has been stated that because of the waywardness of his course in the sky he is more independent and hence more powerful than the sun; he is also the god who restores men's energies during the night.[7] At any rate, whatever the reason may have been, he was regarded as a controlling factor in the growth of vegetation and so influenced the month and year of the calendar, features we miss among the Assyrians, who started the day at sunrise. But beyond this difference they made no important change. The moon god's main sanctuary was at Ur. Shamash, the sun god, was responsible for light, for well-being among men and also for justice, a concept that approached the Egyptian ma'at as the social and legal manifestation of the cosmic order of things. He saw all and knew all, but unlike Yahweh, who meted out punishment to every individual for his acts of unrighteousness, he delegated to the ruler the right to act in accordance with the law; it was he who handed down the code of laws to Hammurabi. This was, however, not the only function of the sun god; when his mid-day rays scorched the crops and the backs of men or brought disease, this heavenly body was under the influence of another deity. The chief temple of the sun god was at Larsa. Nergal, who in early times had functioned in the world above, had descended to the lower world, where, after emerging with success from a combat with its queen, he married her and took over her kingdom. As a deity identified with the hot rays of the sun, with pestilence, which was, in popular opinion, caused by the heat of the sun, with after-life, which was by no means cheerful—as a power associated with death and conditions leading to death, his influence on man was regarded as anything but beneficial. All souls must eventually come into his kingdom, a dark, gloomy realm where men, unless properly buried and provided for, would have to eat dust and

7. M. Jastrow: *The Religion of Babylonia and Assyria*, Boston, 1898, p. 304.

drink foul water. There was no hope of continuing on as one
had lived above, as in Egypt, which partially accounts for the
less carefully constructed tombs, although the Mesopotamians
did lay emphasis on proper burial. There are occasional intima-
tions about a division between a place reserved for exceptional
people and a region of more severe punishments, but apparently
no man allowed himself to be carried away by a dream of the
Elysian Fields.

The Sumerian goddess of creation, called Nintu or Ninharsag,
introduced a concept into cosmic generation which was destined
to have far-reaching consequences in the later Near East and
Greece. Like the motion of a whirlpool, the whirlwind, the
spider and the silkworm and the supposedly rotating shadow of
the moon, this divinity whirled herself into being, at the same
time throwing off enough energy to create and support life
around her. Where can we find a parallel so much like the spiral
of nuclear and nebular energy, that can bridge the gap so well
between the ancient's version of the origin of life and similar
attempts of modern science? Once she appears as an anthropomorphic spindle capable of supplying her own motive power,
then as a figure whirling the spindle in her own hands. She
furnished early Greek philosophy with the vortex and be-
queathed the spinning Aphrodite to later religion. What this
people lacked in logical acumen they made up for by way of
fertile imagination.

Ishtar, the only outstanding female in the whole pantheon,
was a goddess of fertility—in the soil, in man and beast; she
was the power inherent in all life which apparently lies dormant
at times but renews itself at certain set intervals. The sacred
harlots in her temple at Erech, undoubtedly a survival of a
more primitive time, were thought of as a symbolical encouragement to keep this life-giving force throbbing for the benefit of
man, regardless of what the moralizing Herodotus and the
modern may have thought about the practice.[8] She was a god-

---

8. I, 199.

dess of love who hesitated at nothing to attain the satisfaction of her desire, not even the destruction of her lovers. She had to descend each year to the underworld and remain there for a season, where she was stripped of her clothing and insulted by the consort of Nergal before she returned to the upper world.[8a] It may seem strange to the modern that with all this emphasis on resurrection in nature, no doctrine of resurrection for man ever suggested itself to the Mesopotamian to still the longing for immortality running through the Gilgamesh epic, but this is a subject we must take up again later. To obtain satisfaction for desire often brings struggle and strife from the lowest creature to the level of man, and so Ishtar included war in her province of patronage; the original significance of her sword, however, was astronomical, from which the association with war was derived. Nabu, originally a water deity associated with Ea, was the god of wisdom, but a wisdom undoubtedly of a practical nature. Water flowing through the canals to nourish the fields exercised a certain magic tantamount, in Babylonian thinking, to wisdom; this concept was evidently no more abstract than the justice of Shamash. Under the supremacy of Babylon's Marduk, Nabu, whose shrine was in neighboring Borsippa, became the son of his rival, still maintaining, however, an enviable position in the pantheon. Under the Assyrian Semiramis, who eventually became a misplaced star in the diadem of modern romance, he took on a new lease on life in a new quarter, but little is known about this queen's preference for the god of wisdom.[9] A number of other divinities such as Ramman, a god of thunder and war, assumed a relative importance without adding anything significant to the overall picture of Mesopotamian religion.

Marduk, originally a god of the rising sun, rose to a pre-

8a. There are two versions of this story, one in which the Sumerian Inanna plays the leading role, while Ishtar figures in a later version (S. N. Kramer: *Sumerian Mythology,* Philadelphia, 1944, pp. 84-96).

9. A. T. Olmstead (*op. cit.,* pp. 165-66) compares the worship of Nabu with that of Aton by Akhenaton of Egypt.

eminent position in the pantheon along with the fortunes of
Babylon and remained there as long as the city held her own
in the valley. He became the hero of the gods by overcoming
the dread Tiamat and establishing universal order on a firm
basis. His large temple, Esagila, which housed his statue of gold,
shrines dedicated to other divinities, and the law code of Hammurabi, became a national center of worship, the focal point of
the New Year's festival celebrated in the god's honor. The worship of this divinity may be hailed as an approach to mono-
theism, though far from anything akin to that of the Hebrews.[10]
Far from annihilating other divinities, he climbed up from one
shoulder to another to the peak of a hierarchy which continued
to give him support. As a creator of man and the world he was
close to the heart of every citizen, much closer than Amon-Ra
of Thebes, especially close to the ruler because Marduk was the
guardian of the political welfare of the kingdom. As late as
539 B.C., when the Persians captured the city, Cyrus cites Marduk
as his divine benefactor. Ashur, an early national god of the
Assyrians, is another divinity raised to the peak of a hierarchy
and lost sight of after the fall of Nineveh in 612 B.C. Despite the
respect paid to Babylonian deities by Assyrian monarchs, their
national pride dictated allegiance to this god of war whose
image was carried on a standard into battle. Beneath the head
of the pantheon the Assyrians ranked other divinities from the
south, especially Ishtar who enjoyed a popular shrine at Arbela.
The image of Ashur with its arrows and quiver and winged disc
became a model for the Persian artist of a later date, when he
applied the same attributes to his god Ahura-Mazda. The
Assyrians, whose time was taken up largely with waging war,
raised their prayers both to Ashur and Ishtar as gods of the
battlefield who, as history tells us, seldom disappointed them.

In what relation did the ruler of Mesopotamia stand to his
divinity? Most authorities seem to agree that he was the representative of divinity on earth, a chosen vessel that still had to

---

10. Consult E. A. W. Budge: *Babylonian Life and History*, London,
1925, p. 101.

search out the wishes of the gods as best he could before taking them into account in practice.[11] Divinity was only conferred upon certain rulers posthumously. This fact spells an important distinction between Mesopotamia and Egypt, where the pharaoh was an acknowledged divinity. There is no doubt that a close relationship existed in nearly all oriental countries between religion and politics, but where the ruler is an avowed divinity, the control of succession, the dictation of policy and the allocation of funds must fall under the sway of a god-king and priests who can always wield, in the name of the ruler, the strong whip of revelation with effectiveness. In Mesopotamia both priest and king were on the same human level, cut off permanently from a family association with the divinity, both subject to the same laws of mortality. Even if a priest was in a better position to ferret out the whims of a god and perhaps frighten people into submission with his findings, his word had nothing of the compelling force of an Egyptian ruler who, as god and man, could be made manifest to his people in all his glory, whose infallible dictates, descending through governors and officials, apparently superseded a code of law. The Sumerian ensi of the early period was often a priest as well, whereas later, especially in Assyria, the ruler was frequently the son of the former king; we know too that the Assyrian monarch was superstitious enough to be very dependent on the interpretations of the priest, but all this was of less consequence in the face of the line of separation between god and man. Nor does the fact that certain prominent persons were buried with all manner of luxurious equipment, as in the "Royal Tombs" of Ur, bring man any nearer to an identification with divinity. We have already mentioned that

---

11. M. Jastrow: *op. cit.,* p. 374. Assyrian kings called themselves sons of Ashur, but this is only an expression of attachment (*ibid.,* p. 200); E. A. W. Budge: *op. cit.,* p. 160; P. Carlton (*op. cit.,* pp. 91, 129, 183ff.) mentions rulers who assumed the title of divinity but were moved by a desire to hold a federated group together by a spirit of nationalism; H. Frankfort (*Kingship and the Gods,* Chicago, 1948, p. 237) emphasizes the difference between the divine Pharaoh and the "divine burden" of a Mesopotamian ruler.

Cyrus credited his success in capturing Babylon to the favors showered upon him by Marduk; and in so doing he appealed to the hearts of the people, who regarded their god as a national divinity. So far as we know, neither Cyrus nor Cambyses resorted to a self-deification as a method of controlling people anywhere in the course of their conquests, and the latter was not astute enough to use the same strategy in Egypt which Alexander later adopted to be acknowledged the rightful descendant of the pharaohs.

The major divinities, once they were established in their respective communities, were given consorts, who, in some cases, were granted shrines contiguous to the city's chief temple. Some of these consorts were arbitrarily chosen without attaching much significance to their names; some, who had been male, became female and others, like the wife of Nergal, were debased divinities. Fathers and sons, though their connections apparently had some original significance, were juggled about to suit political convenience. The gods, they believed, ought to have some family organization, but the behavior of one god to another offered no commendable precedent for a respectable family among men. Divinities were further classified in general groups: the Igigi, or gods of heaven, and the Ananuki, or gods of the earth, the latter being far more numerous. This classification seems to have had no other purpose than convenience; it may also have helped to be sure all were included in a petition and that no offense would be given by a possible omission. The chief divinities were also represented by the planets: Marduk was associated with Jupiter, Ishtar with Venus, Nergal with Mars, Nabu with Mercury, and Ninib, an Assyrian war god, with Saturn. Aside from the major divinities there were countless demons and devils, most of them evil in nature, and as a class, more numerous because of the inseparable gap between gods and men. These creatures, most of whose names were unknown, took the form of a dragon, a serpent, and other beasts of a horrible shape and appeared especially in destructive winds. Other demons brought diseases of every nature. Strange as it may seem, these creatures, created by the gods to plague mankind, were exorcised by the priests in the name of a major divinity, another testimony to the unmoral character of Mesopotamian gods. Evil demons frequently took up their residence in witches or used the evil eye for weaving a spell of magic to the detriment of the victim; to rid oneself of a disease or spell the priest was consulted or summoned to the sick man's bedside.

Magic, then, was as prevalent, if not more common, in Mesopotamian religion than in most religions of the ancient east. The most common form was divination, an effort to learn what was in the mind of a god before any future undertaking or event. Here again the priest, with his specialized knowledge, was indispensable. Night after night the heavens were carefully observed for the position of stars and planets in their relation to the moon and other heavenly bodies. Any peculiar manifestation was recorded, compared with records of the past, interpreted by priests, and reported to the ruler. The animal sacrificed was carefully watched and its entrails closely examined; the liver, which carried most weight with the diviner, was the subject of special attention. The movements of animals and birds had their peculiar meaning, above all, anything unusual in the way of an eclipse, an earthquake, or unseasonal phenomenon might portend unfavorable consequences. Often great undertakings were postponed indefinitely until the powers above revealed their will through favorable omens.[12] Another branch of magic was applied to the healing of the sick, wherein we again find a strange combination of common sense and primitive superstition. They knew something about the properties of herbs to be administered to the patient, but the emphasis was laid on magical devices to drive the evil demon from the body; for this, as we have pointed out, they resorted to the priest. The latter, clad in appropriate garments, identified himself with one of the major divinities as he recited an incantation, in some cases resorting to a sacrifice, to the burning of an effigy of the demon or hanging up some form of apotropaic charm in the room of

---

12. Dreams were sometimes invoked by a period of fasting and then interpreted by experts who knew how to distinguish between the favorable and the unfavorable.

the sick man. Man's entire environment was peopled by spirits whose ways could be divined if only he knew how to interpret the visible tokens of phenomena. Once a magician had met with success, in prophecy or a cure, the whole case was recorded and added to similar cases, until a vast storehouse of such documents was compiled. Naturally, as among so many primitives, when failure followed upon the attempt, the fault was ascribed either to inaccuracy in carrying out the prescription or to the weakness of man's perception.

The temple in a Mesopotamian city was the central organ of life, from which the arteries carried forth information and inspiration, whose veins returned with the first fruits of man's every effort. Privileged to reach out into the peasant's fields, into the business man's coffers, its courtyards and chambers saw people going to and fro throughout the day, bent on some religious, political, judicial, or business mission. The temples of the early period were modestly small, usually located within the sacred precinct and near the ziggurat, but with the growth of empire a more spacious dwelling was laid out for the god's ever expanding economy. In general, most temples contained a large chamber housing the god's statue, sometimes of gold, surrounded by chapels dedicated to minor divinities and rooms at the disposal of the priests; a large courtyard containing a basin of water was also included. There was a couch on which the divinity might recline, a boat for his water journeys, an altar for the sacrifice of animals, and quarters for the priests whose number, if we can judge from the duties they fulfilled, must have been very high. Besides moving outside the precinct to perform their offices among the sick, they observed the stars, superintended all other forms of divination, were in charge of sacrifices, kept the financial records in order, and supervised the festivals. They were authorities in the highest type of knowledge, namely that which passed down from god to man. The worship of a god included hymns, rituals, pouring of libations, sacrifices, and the burning of incense, in the course of which the priests no doubt changed their garments a number of times.

As in so many eastern temples, the interior, sheltering the core of religious mysteries, received more attention than the outer walls, which were plain, if not forbidding in comparison. The borderline between what we call the spiritual and the material, if it existed at all, must have been an elastic one, for an outside observer might have mistaken the temple for the banking center of the city; the priests loaned money and controlled a great deal of land, which they administered for the support of the temple. The laws of Hammurabi were set up in the temple of Babylon, which means this institution may have figured prominently in legal matters; it certainly served as a repository for all literary records compiled by the scribes.

The religious expression of this people was inspired largely by fear. The life of man was hemmed in from above by capricious gods who acknowledged little moral responsibility toward their creatures on earth, and by demons full of evil intent for the human slave brought into being for the convenience of divinity. Life after death provided small guarantee of a relief from the tribulations of the present. In the midst of his blind groping for some improvement in his condition, he leaned heavily on magic to satisfy his craving for certainty—magic which has an inevitable way of increasing in direct proportion to the fear in the heart of man. Occasionally he seemed to realize he had committed a wrong in the sight of divinity, but he was sure neither of the particular god's identity nor how he had offended a divinity to whom he confessed vaguely in times of distress and whose compassion he hoped he might somehow touch. There was a change of heart on the part of divinity when mankind was in danger of extermination by the flood, but this compassion of Ishtar, a goddess whose interests were closely identified with those of man, was apparently dictated more by expediency than by personal sympathy with his plight. The latter lived as much as possible within the dictates of divine approval because he knew of no safety elsewhere. He cried out in affliction but experienced nothing of what we call repentant conversion. It may seem surprising that he never resorted to the deification of the ruler, as in Egypt, or to the intercession of a mediator from on high, but these are questions we must reserve until later.

Before the middle of the past century Rawlinson succeeded in deciphering the trilingual inscription which the Persian Darius had left on the rock of Behistun, and in doing so he furnished a key to another literature of the past. The compact character of cuneiform script and the cheap writing materials available enabled the Mesopotamian to turn out more writing than any other ancient people, but the use of fragile clay has also brought about, in the course of time and excavations, the destruction of a large number of records. A vast number turned out to be commercial and magical in character, little of which can be listed in the category of literature. In a community where the majority of people were illiterate, the scribe was bound to find plenty of employment in both writing and reading, arts he had learned in childhood while attending a school conducted by the priests and connected with the temple. The pupils listened carefully to instructions, then copied from the copious material in the temple library, at the same time memorizing the characters they used. While the calling of the scribe must have been a respected one, we hear less about its dignity than in Egypt; this may be due to the fact that the pictographic characters of the Egyptian language called for a more skilled artist. Once he had completed his training, the scribe might serve the local temple, he might be sent abroad to copy records in other libraries, or take his station in a busy sector where the average citizen would have need of his services. If the scribe was less an artist than in Egypt, we must grant that the respect for the power of the spoken or written word was as binding here as elsewhere. Before Marduk set out to engage Tiamat and her forces in battle, the gods made trial of his spoken word, which, much to their satisfaction, caused a piece of cloth, placed in their midst, to vanish into thin air.[13] From religion the power given to the word by

---

13. J. B. Pritchard: *Ancient Near Eastern Texts*, Princeton, 1950, p. 66.

or through either the speaker or writer supposedly passed on to law and business contracts.

There is hardly a piece of Mesopotamian literature which cannot be called religious, in which the gods, their attributes, their deeds and preferences are not mentioned; and where divinity is not referred to, we can see a god or demon looking over the shoulder of the writer. Much of this writing, drawn from the libraries of temples, is magical in character—incantations, prayers, ritual procedures. Every day had its own ritual and sacrifice in the busy life of the priest; every strange, unusual manifestation, such as an earthquake, the falling of a statue, or unseasonable weather, called forth the ingenuity of the diviner, absorbing much of the life of the priest and worshipper. The bulk of this literature, with its emphasis on exact methods of procedure, is monotonous to the modern reader, with the exception of the prayers, which follow the rhythmical pattern of the distich (prose was the exception rather than the rule). The worshipper who curried the favor of a god first flattered him by rehearsing his attributes, emphasizing his power and majesty, calling to mind past allegiance, reminding him of his connection with the city of the worshipper. In this way he hoped to gain the ear and exclusive attention of the god. Then came the petition, in the course of which the worshipper humbled himself, cajoled and scolded, praised and then made promises for the future. The great god of the sun traversed the expanse of the sky, even down to the ocean's depths, supposedly for man's benefit; he dealt out justice to everyone but would not take on that sympathetic, intimate association with man and nature we have found in the hymn of Akhenaton. The Mesopotamian god held himself aloof from man, his intentions were concealed behind a dark cloud. This groping into the mind of the gods called forth a more widespread use of magic to steal a march on his caprice and to forestall a possible calamity.

The remoteness of divinity gave encouragement to belief in mediatory spirits or demons that assumed a great number of guises. The evil demons, countless in number, were the object of most incantations; because the good spirits failed to inspire fear, they were sadly neglected. When a man was visited by some manner of affliction, the resourceful magician, after making his examination, had to identify himself with a good and supposedly superior force before the mischief-maker could be exorcised by a process often far from pleasant for the patient. In this way he cured disease, cast out devils, averted the evil eye, waged war on witches, employing amulets, images, and disguises to attain his ends. To probe into the future, the priest and monarch took every precaution to circumvent the watchful eye of a fickle divinity or a malicious demon to insure successful results; here again they read from tablets inscribed with incantations and prescriptions appropriate to all occasions, the magician reciting them repeatedly in a dull monotone. The interpretation of dreams and oracles guided monarchs in great undertakings, *e.g.* the building of temples and military expeditions. In all this body of writing the preponderance of fear prevented the individual writer from embellishing his style, and thus literary merit was sacrificed to a painstaking exactness to bring about a practical result. Had divinity been more human and sympathetic, magic would have assumed a minor role, allowing the worshipper to pour forth his praise and blame in more attractive utterances.

The desire to sum up the truth of man's experience in his world has created the admonition or proverb to teach the citizen to follow the path of expediency to a life of greater security. Certain people and actions are to be shunned, while others are commended; certain causes are destined to bring about certain effects. Let every man pay due respect to authority, for a man is lost without his king and queen, his lord and master. Silence in the presence of superiors, modesty and obedience to a lord are stressed. Who would marry a harlot to lift himself out of trouble? Refrain from quarreling, avoid lawsuits, have nothing to do with slander and thievery; not so much because such actions are wrong in themselves but are rather a decided disadvantage in the pursuit of happiness. Do not neglect divinity, for prayer atones for sin and sacrifice prolongs life. Evil is the prerogative of certain spirits constantly trying to snare a man in the trap of deception; good is likewise in the hands of powerful forces, and man must follow rigid general rules to avoid the one and gain the other. Once again, as in Egypt, the fear of the lord is the beginning of all practical wisdom. It may be surprising to some to discover here a foreshadowing of Christian ethics: recompense the evil-doer with good; do no wrong to your enemies; give food, drink, and clothing to those in need—and all this not because one identifies himself with the suffering and misfortune of others but to win favor in the eyes of Shamash, the god of justice. All such teachings are summed up in short staccato sentences completing a full link between cause and effect and passing directly from the negative to the positive; no space is left for exception or equivocation; no quarter is granted to the indifferent; no room given in the middle of the road.

Since catastrophe in the form either of flood and storm or of conquest was a greater threat to personal security than in Egypt, and because divinity was so callous to the heart's appeal, there was more occasion for sorrow and weeping. The temperament of the Mesopotamian was also more heavy and melancholy; there are times when he, like the Hebrew, seems to glory in his sorrow as though it were an indispensable spiritual catharsis. The city of Ur had been sacked and destroyed by its enemies, its temples shattered, its fields overrun, most of its people slain—all of which is the theme of a lengthy lamentation, written in eleven songs, which opens with the original motivation on the divine level. The city, for some reason, had met with the displeasure of Anu and Enlil, who sent an evil calamity upon her, despite the intercession of the city's goddess. The latter, along with the other gods, has quit the temples, apparently as wretched over the calamity as the inhabitants. The poet then descends to the mundane level to describe the effects of the actual disaster: the conquest of the city is portrayed with a bitter realism that leaves no question in the mind of the reader. One has a vague feeling that the poet, unable to find a reason for the calamity, has pictured both gods and men in a sorry plight as a result, a roundabout way of using divinity as a scapegoat for man's infirmities. Toward the end, the poet, still feasting on the dregs of melancholy, petitions the goddess to restore the fortunes of her city, even though her efforts to avert the storm had been futile. There is, of course, no open indictment against divinity whose *modus operandi,* as in magic, is theoretically as right as right can be; hence man's last resort was to present himself in a sorry plight and to include the goddess in the same predicament. With all its repetition, which was more impressive to the ancient than to the modern ear, the poet's emotional description of a hopeless destruction moves us to sympathize with a people who were groping for some kind of meaning in events and meeting with a blank wall, but nevertheless went on striving to maintain a kind of order in their life.

In the hymns and prayers of the so-called Penitential Psalm, we sense again the prostrate humility of the worshipper, his inability to identify his sins, his frantic effort to arouse mercy in the heart of an indifferent god: all men are hopelessly floundering in sin, which may have been inherited from ancestors to bear fruit in the reckless days of youth—sins committed knowingly and unknowingly. The ways of the gods are too high, too obscure for man to fathom; he can only hope vaguely for mercy and purification. In the hymn to Ishtar, the petitioner, like Job, cries out desperately to learn what he has done to offend his superior; in the prayer addressed to every god he appeals indiscriminately to god and goddess, to gods known and unknown for relief; he has constantly looked for help, but no one either gives an ear or lends a hand.[14]

The epic is the most outstanding form of Mesopotamian literature, one in which the writer achieved the nearest approach to the Greek viewpoint. The so-called Creation Epic, because the action includes only divinities, has nothing of the human appeal of the *Iliad* or the *Odyssey,* but it has epic dimensions; there is the same rise of dynamic tension before the great duel; the marshalling of Tiamat's armed forces calls to mind the dream of Agamemnon.[15] The original condition of the universe is pic-

---

14. J. B. Pritchard: *op. cit.,* pp. 391-92.
15. *Iliad,* II, 23–70.

tured as an infinitely large, chaotic mass of waters represented by the male Apsu and his consort Tiamat, who gave birth to the great divinities of the Mesopotamian pantheon, divinities of a lower rank and hence more akin to the finite. The latter bustle about in an attempt to bring order into chaos or, as we may put it, to complement their own imperfections and thus disturb the parents, the advocates of a continued *status quo*. Ea, the resourceful one, succeeds in overpowering Apsu, but Tiamat, who creates a cohort of ugly monsters to support her cause, is another matter. After most of the divinities have been frightened in the face of her forces, Marduk, the powerful and valiant son of Ea, is chosen to lead the gods against the common enemy. In the duel which ensues Marduk slays Tiamat and takes Kingu, her chief ally, captive. Then Marduk establishes limitations to the various parts of the universe, creates man from the blood of Kingu to serve as a slave to the gods, and assigns to various divinities certain spheres of influence. The action of the cosmological drama is unfolded entirely on the plane of the divine, man coming on the stage only to play an incidental role. The mighty characters are very impersonal, with very little *esprit de corps* and, like many of their worshippers, showing little moral responsibility in their mutual relationships. Like man, they seek personal advantage by magic, by flattery, and above all by the use of brute force in pursuing a policy of expediency; once they are masters of the universe they create slaves to keep the earth in order and to insure a certain amount of peace and security for themselves, but the reader feels almost certain that such creatures, so dependent on action to satisfy their greed, will never rest in a state of calm inertia. Though the language is expressive of an epic struggle, the contest is so titanic, so far beyond human conception it leaves one, as in the battle between Milton's God and Satan, overwhelmed with awe but removed from sympathetic participation.

The Gilgamesh story, striking at one of the most fundamental problems haunting human life and thought, enlists the main character on our side in his struggle against overwhelming odds; here we find the early roots of both epic and tragic conflict. The hero, two-thirds god and one-third man, is presented to us as a monarch so powerful and self-sufficient he has little need of gods above and pays little attention to man below his station— a lonesome demigod for whose strength even the pantheon has respect. Complaints were registered against him; the gods then created another giant, Enkidu by name, who was expected to deliver the people from the oppression of Gilgamesh and to avenge his insults to divinity. The new giant was lured from the fields by a harlot, but once in the city of Erech the two giants, while they had one quarrel, soon thereafter became fast friends. They shared a new series of adventures in the midst of which the gods reached down with a hand of warning restraint: first, after Gilgamesh rejected the amorous advances of Ishtar, a powerful bull is sent against them; secondly, the giant Enkidu falls a prey to death. Gilgamesh, now conscious of a great need in his makeup, first mourns for his friend and then sets out on his quest for immortality. At the end of another series of adventures he finds his ancestor Uta-Napishtim, immortal and sequestered on an island, who tells him the story of the flood. No, there is no immortal man, except the Sumerian Noah, for so the gods have decreed. To assuage his melancholy, Gilgamesh is given a plant containing in its juices the powers of rejuvenation, but in this case his stupidity allows it to fall within reach of a serpent. Gilgamesh, now somewhat chastened, continues on his melancholy way homeward, not yet, however, reconciled to the fact of death. Ea brings forth the spirit of Enkidu from the realm below to answer the queries of his friend. The latter learns it is hard to kick against the goad. Although the poem is incomplete, it is difficult to believe there was a subsequent change of fortune to crown the desires and efforts of such a hero.

In contrast to the Creation Epic, the story of Gilgamesh reflects the most telling paradox of human thought and action, a philosophical problem radiating from the background into the concrete words and deeds of the characters. Its language need not strain itself as in the description of the conflict among divinities, for here it deals with its own creator, his joys and sorrows, his ambitions and limitations. The poem is also the earliest presentation of man's development from innocence to self-realization in a world of indifferent circumstances. Regarded in this light, the work may be divided into two sections: the events before and after the death of Enkidu. In the first section Gilgamesh is as self-sufficient as a divinity, unconscious of any void in his life; in the latter part he is a human being whose great need has created a great problem arising from the passing of his friend. He descends to earth where we can understand and sympathize with him.[16] During his early career his exploits rid the land of many a monster and so benefited his fellow man, but Gilgamesh, instead of being aware of his beneficiaries, is more concerned about finding an outlet for his boundless energy. Like Herakles, he seems to act at the behest of some fateful compulsion which he makes no attempt to understand. This adventure for adventure's sake continues into the second section, until he sets out on his journey to his immortal ancestor when such tasks become hindrances on the road to a desired end. Of course, Enkidu became his friend in the first section, but it is only with his death that Gilgamesh is conscious of the value of his friendship for the other man, the creature lured by a harlot from a state of natural blessedness and innocence into the civilization of the city where he meets his downfall; he must be sacrificed before Gilgamesh can grow to full stature as a man.

The lofty strains of the poet become more varied in the second section to reveal the conflict of the inner man as he struggles blindly against the brute force of circumstances; the pale cast of thought throws a gloomy spell over the man of action, but act he must and act he does! It is also interesting to note that as the hero becomes more human, the gods also take on more human traits: they "cowered like dogs crouched against the outer wall of the universe," Ishtar "cried out like a woman in travail," and after the flood, "the gods crowded like flies" around the sacrifice. The gods, through their sufferings, come to feel compassion for their slaves, as self-centered as most of their feelings may be. The reader, however, is not so much drawn

---

16. Cf. G. R. Levy: *The Sword from the Rock*, London, 1953, p. 122.

to the gods who, after the flood, go on their merry way without much consideration for man, as to the hero whose plight in contrast is so much more despairing. The primary reason for this despair is the fear of death which changes his whole outlook after the passing of Enkidu, the physical giant who suffered an unheroic death away from the field of battle. The fact that he, Gilgamesh, like all men, must leave behind the pleasures of a good life and descend to the dark, dusty realms of Nergal, in spite of all his strength and prowess, haunts him to the end of the poem. Yet he, like many a man, goes on struggling against the inevitable. While he evidently envies Uta-Napishtim, he fails to see, as the reader perhaps does see, how dull and uninteresting the life of his immortal ancestor must be, imprisoned on a lonesome island, apart from human society, condemned to a monotonous routine in a framework of sameness like that of "the painted ship upon a painted ocean." And how could a man of action, a lover of adventure fare in such a static prism? No, 'tis better to see Gilgamesh go on searching for what he cannot find, for Uta-Napishtim who condones the sad lot of mortal man was made immortal by a mistake of the gods and may be living, from our standpoint, a very deceptive existence. Although Gilgamesh may appear to the modern somewhat of a brutish, immature child, of all characters in Mesopotamian lore he is the most representative and compelling, the most universally typical both in his glory and self-pitying sadness.

The story of Ishtar and her lover Tammuz is another myth symbolic of the recurring change of seasons, one which includes only divinities. Closely following a ritual pattern such as we find among so many early peoples, it calls for mourning when vegetation dies and rejoicing in the spring; the resurrection from winter was never confined to man. Adapa, the fisherman, broke the wings of the south wind, whereupon he was given an opportunity to make himself immortal and, in this case again, lost out in his quest for immortality, for he was tricked by divinity into making the wrong choice. Another example is Etana, the husband so concerned about his wife's labors in childbirth he ascended to heaven on the back of an eagle to find a magic herb for allaying the woman's suffering; he failed to reach heaven but was saved from a disastrous fall, no doubt by the eagle, which, if we may add an ending to an incomplete text, swooped down to save his rider. Other interesting tales, including that of the Zu bird and Enlil, can add little to our subject which has not already been said.[17] The tales cited here, it must be stressed, bring us face to face with the most significant aspects of man considered in relation to the world at large, and though we of today have pushed many of these problems into the mind's background, the threat of inundation to well-laid plans is still with us; we still depend on the change of seasons, and the fear of death is responsible for much of the apprehension and beauty associated with human living. To the Mesopotamian these problems were more immediate and hence more fraught with fear; he felt himself in closer touch with the eternal prospect of changes as he saw them.

Exactness is a requisite for the writing of laws and therefore one of the reasons for the use of prose instead of verse in early civilizations. The code of Hammurabi, one of the most distinctive contributions of Mesopotamian writing, is far from being the first example recorded; it was based, as we have said, on a number of codes of his predecessors and adapted to his own needs. First, we note a strong class distinction between the aristocrats, freedmen, and slaves, which means the punishment varied according to the social status of the injured: if the latter was a commoner or a slave, punishment usually took the form of a fine; otherwise it might require a death in the family of the accused. There are features decidedly archaic, based on religious superstition, and others which might be considered enlightened measures even in our own times: in certain cases of sorcery and adultery the ordeal was employed; on the other hand, the state, not having furnished ample protection for private property, was required to make good the loss if the robber was not caught.[18] Furthermore, an act of god was regarded as something beyond human control, and whether or

---

17. For the details of such tales consult S. N. Kramer: *Sumerian Mythology*, Philadelphia, 1944.

18. J. B. Pritchard: *op. cit.*, p. 167.

not such a visitation was construed as a punishment from on high, it had no effect in the procedure of law. We also note a great respect for the written word, not only in the emphasis on written contracts but in the fact that the whole code was inscribed on diorite and set up in a public place.

As we should expect in an agricultural community, the rights of the landowner were protected by regulations governing rents, loans, and interest rates, by fixed prices, and it must be remembered that land tended to remain, by inheritance, in the family. The code encouraged trade by guarding the trader against thievery; debtors were dealt with rather harshly; contracts in business were almost sacred. The woman, in her own sphere, enjoyed equal rights with the man both in ownership of property and in marriage; regulations for divorce and dowry put her on an equal social level with her husband. The so-called *lex talionis* made certain punishments, especially for builders and physicians, very severe and out of proportion to the crime committed. Other punishments seem to us somewhat extreme because of the multiple restitution involved. Forgery, false accusation, and above all, false judgment on the part of a judge were severely dealt with. Later the influence of such a code spread to the Hebrews.[19] The framing and enforcement of the code was ultimately the responsibility of the king, which no doubt explains why there is so little mention of the divine in the code itself, but we must bear in mind that the king was responsible to the divinity; the code, taken by itself, may seem entirely secular but actually it is far from being divorced from religion. In the prologue the king boasts in lavish language of what he has done for god and man, and in the epilogue he curses, in the name of every powerful god, the one who may dare to efface the inscribed stele. There is little doubt that the seated figure at the top of the stele is Shamash, the god of justice, the standing figure Hammurabi, receiving the code from his god.

In Mesopotamia, especially in the southern part of the valley, stone suitable for architectural purposes was a rarity, and

---

19. Exodus 21:24-27.

therefore brick became the common building material. These bricks were largely sun-dried, first of a plano-convex shape, later more square, and usually stamped by the builder, a fact which is a decided asset for dating. To compensate for the lack of strength which only stone can give, walls were made massive and so brick buildings gave the impression of being just as strong, if not stronger, than stone structures; what's more, the use of brick permitted the architect to depart from the more rigid, straight lines of the lintel system in favor of the curve forming the arch, the vault, and possibly the dome. Besides furnishing an interesting variation in line, more space was given to the interior and more vitality to the structure seen from within. For binding the bricks together they used, first, mud mixed with straw, and later bitumen, of which they had a rich supply, and lime mortar, which proved to be the most durable. When stone was required for any special purpose, it had to be transported from a distance. Wood was also a rare article, but because many rulers had easy access to Lebanon, it was frequently used for ceilings and doorposts. The metal worker, plying his craft in gold, silver, and copper contributed little to architecture.

The walls of the temples were exceedingly thick, so thick the spaces enclosed by them must have taken on an appearance of secondary importance. Such an overwhelming display of strength, such a continuous line of brick surface would have cowed the observer at close range and struck him as monotonous from a distance, had it not been for towers, still more massive gateways, and wall decorations in the form either of painted plaster or glazed bricks. In spite of the brilliant coloring the temple complex was like a huge pachyderm in a Siberian tundra, reduced by its bulk to a state of helpless motionlessness; today what remains of these walls are as drab as the landscape around them. Such walls surrounded the temple enclosures, which included the main temple, the ziggurat, and sometimes the ruler's palace. Most of the structures on the ancient sites were so thoroughly destroyed it is difficult to reconstruct them; in most cases, however, the temple had two courts, one outside for the people in general, one inside reserved for the priests and the king who

was also, in a certain sense, a priest as well, and a holy of
holies, beyond the inner court, containing the statue of the
divinity; along the sides ran a series of rooms designed for
chapels, records, storage purposes, dwellings for priests, and
stalls for sacrificial animals, for the citizen regarded this building
as a community center for religion, business, and the dispen-
sation of justice. In early Sumerian times the dimensions were
comparatively modest, but with the construction of Marduk's
Esagila in Babylon our respect increases for the Mesopotamian
architect and his building, which must have been mammoth
and the number of rooms legion, all supported by an extensive
platform that had to be laid down in the soft soil before the
building proper was begun. We note too that here, as in Egypt,
the secrets of the inner shrine were shrouded in mystery, shut
off from the eye of the common man, because religion and its
ritual sought to deny the unpredictability of changing circumstances outside the temple walls.

The most distinctive and the best preserved feature of this
architecture was the ziggurat, the high tower rising above the
rest of the precinct. It too rested upon a solid foundation, rising
by somewhat clumsy, rectangular stages to the top, which was
often surmounted by a small temple. Instead of a steady development from stages to a smoothly sloping ascent, as in the
pyramids, one level squats solidly on the other throughout its
architectural history as if loath to forget the earth from which
it rises. Far from soaring into space it keeps its cumbersome
stages in position by sheer weight; the stairways, ascending in
broken lines like ramps, tend to accentuate the control of the
horizontal over the vertical. There is no typical ziggurat; beyond
the general features already mentioned, there were variations
in size, proportion, number of stages, and stairways.[20] A comparison with the Egyptian pyramid only emphasizes the differences between the two. There is certainly little trace of any
architectural influence passing between the two lands, nor was
the original purpose of these structures the same. The height

---

20. For the variations in lower Mesopotamia consult A. Parrot: *Ziggurats et Tour de Babel,* Paris, 1949, pp. 156-57.

of the ziggurat was generally less than that of the pyramid; the former turned its four corners to the cardinal directions, while the latter faced them with its sides; the ziggurat fails to achieve a point, the top surface usually reserved for a small temple; the ascent was no matter of interest to the builder of the pyramid; in Egypt this towering structure dwarfs the accompanying temple, while the ziggurat may have been merely the original base for a temple. To understand fully the differences between the two, a deeper insight into the viewpoints of these two peoples is necessary.

What can the archaeologist tell us about the purpose of the ziggurat? It is dangerous to think of it as a tomb, for although one was found to contain a chamber, this one fact barely argues in favor of a mortuary building. Nor is it likely that the Mesopotamians set it up as a mountain or lofty place of worship simply because they had come from a mountainous country. In the first place, we know too little about the origin of the Sumerians, and even if they came from a land of high mountains, they are not the only people who preferred to worship in high places and who regarded mountains as sacred sites suitable for the manifestation of divinity. One might say it was a gateway to the other world (certainly not the world of the dead below), that it was a symbol of the whole earth, a temporary residence for a god or a place for the celebration of the sacred marriage (which may explain the presence of a couch in the temple on the summit), or an astrological observatory for the practice of divination. There is a possibility in each of these suggestions, but no single one is cogent enough to eliminate the others. It may have been regarded as a connecting link between heaven and earth, along which man could ascend to meet the divinity or to permit the divinity to descend to the earth, but all this fails to go beyond probability.[21] All one can be sure of is the urge on the part of early peoples to bridge the gap between man and divinity and, in the light of the Gilgamesh epic, this urge was at once the hope and despair of this particular people. Much as they realized how unconcerned the gods were about

21. A. Parrot: *op. cit.*, p. 211.

man's ultimate welfare, the Mesopotamians knew they would be completely lost without their occasional interference into human affairs and without an opportunity to anticipate the designs of the gods for the future. This height, rising up in the midst of a level valley, gave man an opportunity to peer into what was beyond his understanding and attainment and was also a standing invitation to divinity to turn his face to man below.

The best example of a palace is that of the Assyrian Sargon at Khorsabad. The general impression of this structure, from a distance, must have been that of a huge, sprawling colossus hugging the level plain like a turtle on the ocean floor; not even the ziggurat nearby did much to counteract the depressing flatness. An extensive artificial mound was first prepared for the superstructure, the outside faced with solid blocks of stone, which was more plentiful here than in the south. Above the heavy platform, the greater part of the walls was composed of brick, with the exception of the lining and certain portions of the columns, where stone was used. The outside wall of the structure, from the bottom of the platform to the very top, measured sixty feet, the height and mass of which must have been overwhelming to the nearby observer. In all, it spread over about twenty-five acres and included about seven hundred rooms, some long and narrow, some square—all arranged around large open courts. Since there was no place in the walls for windows, the lighting and fresh air must have come in from above. The whole palace and its adjacent buildings were well provided with drain pipes. In general, the interior was divided into three parts: the king's quarters, the harem, and the service apartments, with a large open court provided for each section. Along one side was a ramp, probably reserved for the king himself, and at the main entrance was a stairway leading up from opposite directions to the man-headed guardian bulls flanking the main portal. Nearly all the features of these palaces, we know, can be traced to the earlier cities of the south, its greater size alone being the main Assyrian contribution; this people plundered the field of art like the cities of their military victims. The construction of an Assyrian palace required a good share of a monarch's reign, and in some cases he never enjoyed his residence because he was constantly abroad subduing his enemies or he died before it was completed.

Domestic architecture, compared with the temple precinct, was relatively unimportant, one house having been occupied over and over and one after another built on the same site. Below the foundations of brick were frequently graves provided with food and other conveniences for the next life. The rooms, also of brick, were arranged around a central court; they reached up, among the more prosperous, to a height of three and four stories.[22] Some were round, perhaps going back to the old reed hut, while others were rectangular in shape, and all were equipped with excellent draining facilities. Because the evidence is so difficult to interpret, the problem of the roofing has called forth a long debate among the authorities, and this applies to all types of building in Mesopotamia. The roofs were reconstructed flat until a relief from Sennacherib's palace in Nineveh revealed, for the first time, a number of domelike superstructures on a few crowded buildings; now Baldwin Smith suggests these domes were constructed not of masonry but of wood and supplied with a metal covering.[23] If the rooms of Sargon's palace and other Mesopotamian structures were roofed with vaults and domes, regardless of the material used, we can see how they relieved the monotonous lines and angles of the exterior and added considerably to the spaciousness of the interior; it would have, however, detracted little from the general impression of flatness in the building as a whole. The dome can serve as a means of centralization in so many of the churches of the east, but what could it contribute to a complex of buildings or even a private dwelling in which the courtyard takes up so much space and the walls are so cumbersome?

The lack of adequate material explains, first of all, the preponderance of relief sculpture in Sumerian art and also the

---

22. Herodotus, I, 180.

23. *The Dome,* Princeton, 1950, p. 8. The Nineveh relief he believes is a representation of the hilly country of Syria, not of the flat Mesopotamian valley (p. 62).

comparatively small figures done in the round; the usual materials for the latter were limestone, alabaster, and marble. Most of the figures, standing or seated, represent short, squat men and women with large, solidly-blocked-out heads, very short necks, sinewy hands folded across powerful chests, and feet planted firmly on the ground. The law of frontality means as much here as in Egypt, but the contours and modeling separate the two schools by a wide margin. The eyebrows, beneath a low, receding forehead, spread out in opposite directions in sweeping arcs enclosing eyesockets almost triangular in early examples but more almond-shaped in later figures. Whether the eyes are of the same material or lost, leaving two huge caverns, they are far too large for the face, a fact which also applies to the ears. A smooth, almost semicircular line encloses cheek with chin without interruption from the cheekbone, squeezing the features between a heavy brow and a solid, ponderous chin framing the mouth with its half-mocking grin that seeks to belie the staring bewilderment, the melancholy consternation of the eyes above. Perhaps we are reading too much into the face or we should put certain distortions down as attempts to give more expression to the face, but there is no question about the dynamic power in the upper part of the torso, the lively awareness behind the eyes, or the general impression of a solid weight anchored in the foundations of the earth. The figure may be uncertain and trembling with apprehension, or simply innocent in its expectancy; at times it may be as certain as the rock of ages; the body, however, is a potential dynamo of action prepared to go on trying at all odds. Some characters look weird and bizarre; others, because of the folded hands, seem humbly pious, while some are self-satisfied, even overbearing; the whole figure, frank and positive to the extreme, makes no apology for blatant obviousness. Life in this valley was a constant heroic struggle against fear from within and all manner of impediments without.

The group of statues found at Tell Asmar and now in the Louvre were done by a man who was groping vaguely for proportion and some kind of expression in the face; in these and later figures one can never be as sure of his interpretation of features as in the Egyptian statues of the Old Kingdom. The alabaster statue of an official, found at Mari and now in the Louvre, presents a man who no doubt wants to be all he pretends to be, trying to look out farther than his hands can reach, but, despite the strength of his body, he has nothing of the unquestionable self-assurance of the village chieftain of the Nile valley. There are pious little fellows smiling with an air of benediction like preachers blessing the morning offering—but we cannot be too sure! Another figure, also from Mari, stares hollow-eyed from beneath brows dug deeply into the forehead like a sad clown vainly trying to put his best foot forward. The alabaster statuette of a seated lady in the Louvre might very well be a "gemütliche sitzende Hausfrau," were it not for the uneasy tension drawing her well-built body into a nervous knot as she holds on for dear life to the vase before her. The half figure of a male in the British Museum has gone a long way toward the Gudea figures; the modeling is much smoother and more expressive of the inner control over outward manifestations, in short, a better integration achieved by rhythm of line and a more even distribution of masses.

In relief, in which the Mesopotamian felt himself more at home, we find more change and development, perhaps also because of the number of invasions in the land. The Sumerian was certainly not an inspired worker in this medium; this may be due to a poverty of material or to the limitations in the subject matter prescribed by the temple authorities. The Louvre relief of Urnanshe, like so many others, records a matter-of-fact offering of a king and his family, all lined up for display on a festive occasion. Here too the heads and the lower part of the bodies are in profile, while the eyes, somewhat bow-shaped, and the upper torso are full-face to the observer. The figures have overcrowded the available space; each one, except for the king who is the center of attention, expresses the same attitude; each character is very obvious about his part in the spectacle, the purpose of everyone supposedly concentrated on an act of religious devotion. The role of man apparently looms up so large there is no room for background. Something of the same singleness of purpose, but expressed with more assertive power, is found in the vulture stele, portraying King Eannatum in victorious triumph over his enemy. The problem of perspective is dealt with crudely but effectively enough as we see the king's men peering out over their shields arranged compactly in a phalanx and in serried ranks above one another, in both cases looking fixedly ahead to the leader. The forward movement of the army is slow and sluggish—the action is apparently bogged down by the weight of the figures—but as powerfully inevitable as the flow of lava from an active volcano. Beyond this undercurrent of momentum there is little to attract the eye in the flat treatment and obvious statement of predestined events. In the Naram-Sin stele, which ushers in the Akkadians, we are aware of a truth already explicit in Sumerian relief, namely that in the life of these men there is both a subject pushed forward by a concentrated desire and an object to be overcome, but in Sumerian treatment the latter is no more than an incidental detail in the subject's perspective; here we find the enemy capable of moving in a surrounding landscape. The bodies of the warriors are taller and more slender but just as convincing in their steam-rolling power. The observer feels a certain ingenuity as well as power is demanded in this conflict, something of the Theseus of Athenian tradition in preference to the bare brawn of Herakles. The two sides of the triangular mountain emphasize the dramatic stress from each side of the conflict, they suggest a norm against which the contest can be judged and, above all, bring out the stalwart figure of the king in bolder relief.[24] In Egypt, where the regularity of the straight line dominates figure and scene, this background would have meant little, but here, where the power of human energy becomes explicit in a dramatic contest, the backdrop is more than effective in emphasizing the crescendo of the conflict. At first sight this relief, with its landscape and lithe figures, may seem a sharp departure from preceding Sumerian work, but, viewed from the standpoint

---

24. Cf. H. A. Groenewegen-Frankfort: *Arrest and Movement*, London, 1951, pp. 163-64.

of power expression which is the *leitmotif* in the Mesopotamian's struggle with circumstances, the Naram-Sin stele is a more subtly pronounced advance on the same theme.

The peak in monumental sculpture is scaled in the larger figures of Gudea of Lagash. Diorite was brought in from a distance to fashion a statue almost life-size, in the conventional pose of the worshipper standing before his divinity or seated with a flat tablet over the knees; the tablet too is a kind of votive offering to divinity. The power is again obviously restrained, perhaps so much more impressive because, reined in so successfully, the figure achieves a remarkable balance and composure, a control over inexhaustible, physical energy. One need only compare the tiny statuette of the seated woman, already referred to, with the upper section of a lady in diorite in the Louvre to see that the latter is much more at ease, all of which is effected by finer modeling of muscular masses and a more rhythmic treatment of line in accessories. The posing of Gudea is conventional: the head is squarely blocked out; the figure stands or sits most obviously before the spectator; and both the nude surface and the drapery have been treated with a view to creating a whole effect; inscriptions are added to flat surfaces where they interfere the least. As long as religion exerted such a strong influence it would have been impossible for the sculptor to arrive at a greater refinement in conjunction with native simplicity in the presentation of a sinewy titan "fearfully and wonderfully made."

The resourceful imagination of the artist achieved its highest mark in the foundation figurines, so-called, designed to increase the prosperity of the city and therefore placed in boxes beneath the towers of the city wall. To illustrate the spiral motion of creation, the cone or the shadow of the moon was placed in the hands of a genial, elfin figure, somewhat like a character from a Grimm Märchen, who turns the cone, at the same time placing one knee against its lower section to steady the whirling body. The simile then takes on the form of a whirling female, a lady raising both arms aloft to grasp a whorl on her head; the whorl affords an excellent handle for whirling her own body and also steadies her circling motion. Eventually the legs of the female are replaced with the point of the spindle to render the picture more completely persuasive. These bronze figurines served as conveyors of good fortune for the inhabitants of the city; as dynamos of self-created energy they expressed an ideal of motive power, the antithesis of the static line of the Egyptian.

The next significant work in sculpture is the basalt relief above the famous law code of Hammurabi. It unites in its field the Sumerian and Akkadian traditions in that it presents to us heavy, stolid figures occupying a definite place and, from the latter school, it brings a welcome spaciousness which helps us to sense the contrast between the seated Shamash and the royal worshipper receiving the code; from the standpoint of style it looks way ahead to the Persian reliefs of Persepolis. The relationship between god and man is symbolically stressed very much as in the prologue of the code; in the epilogue the king sits on the seat of authority and deals arbitrarily with his subjects. The god, seated in a conventional manner, reaches to the same level as the head of the standing king; although this is not the first instance, the eye of the king, represented in profile in a face raised to high relief, is an agreeable surprise. We note too the repeated occurrence of the horizontal line from the horns to the beard, finally flaring out broadly in the lower garment of the god to emphasize the seated posture in contrast to the flowing vertical lines of the king's dress. We know that law was molded to answer practical demands, but, theoretically, revelation in the form of law descended from god to man; under the aegis of this religious dictate, the sculptor could scarcely improve on the subject of this stele.

In Assyrian relief work, which represents a new trend in material and subject matter, the divinity is so far removed from man he presides only as a symbol or appears by proxy. This art, confined almost entirely to relief, is pictorial, so much so the artist will repeat conventional practices, disregard the rules of perspective, employ exaggerations, and allow the inscription to run straight across the scene—all to produce a picture the observer can easily grasp. One can very well call them pictorial annals with an accompanying cuneiform commentary. Here we must be reminded that such sculpture, so low in relief and so flat to the modern observer, required the addition of color for its full effect. Ashurnazirpal records his military exploits, including his battles on land and river, the siege of cities, the brutal punishment of the enemy, and triumphal processions as well as his hunting excursions. One man is much like another except for accessories. The eyes again are in profile; the muscles of arms and legs are overdone; horses are so stereotyped they resemble rocking horses whose legs never move from one position. The wild beast alone approaches a faithful study from nature. Not only are space relations violated but time is also made more compact for narrative purposes: the outcome of an engagement in the future is adjacent to and in the same framework as the conflict of the present, a device which points ahead to the Romans.

The artists of Sennacherib attempted an advance in two directions: first, they spread the subject over a much wider panorama, thus avoiding too much emphasis on mere episodes; they also experimented with perspective to give more illusion to the receding background, but this, for the most part, only made things more difficult for the observer. We see men dragging a man-headed bull from the quarry, Sennacherib holding an improvised court while his ministers report on a campaign, soldiers fighting in the marshes—a scene mostly documentary in character. Ashurbanipal neglected the battlefield in favor of the hunt, concentrating on small scenes not too much concerned with problems of perspective. There are times when the prostrate animals seem to be lying on a surface which mounts up on an angle sloping from the horizontal to the vertical; moreover, the barren space between the victims seems to put them at a greater disadvantage in the face of rapidly moving chariots. In the portrayal of individual animals the artist reveals his superiority: the lion, bristling with defiance as he leaves his cage, the lioness roaring at her attacker although her hindquarters are paralyzed, the mare looking pathetically back at her offspring —sensitive touches amounting almost to irony when we read the accounts of royal hunting exploits. Otherwise, convention reigns with very little sign of genuine drama to interrupt the steady flow of successive pictorial scenes. One lonesome example, somewhat baroque in its stress on decorative detail, presents the king and queen feasting in the midst of peaceful splendor, attended on one side by a number of servants. The domestic interlude is most persuasive until one catches sight of the head of an Elamite leader suspended within full view of the king, a grim reminder of another sad attempt at rebellion. The Assyrian goes down feasting on cruel brutality.

Color played a prominent role in Mesopotamian art, especially in the jewelry found in the royal cemetery of Ur, and yet painting never achieved more than a subordinate rank. Murals, such as they were, and other wall decorations were concerned mainly with design, and at times the subject was repeated over and over; what is more, the animals in the friezes were stylized and painted in gaudy, unnatural colors. The decorations, which took the form of glazed brick, were designed to relieve the monotonous surface of walls and gateways, the finest example coming from the Ishtar gate of Nebuchadnezzar's Babylon. The potter, who had ample material at his disposal, was a prolific producer in stone and clay, by hand or on the wheel, but very few vases show any interesting examples of painting.[25]

Had the modern found himself in Mesopotamian surroundings, in a climate where the sun beat down with a torrid, humid heat on his back, where storms came up unexpectedly out of a wrathful sky and ruined the fruits of his toil, where an enemy might swoop down from three possible directions to spread carnage in his wake, he might well have despaired of the existence of a divine being—but not the Mesopotamian! Going on in his patient way to keep as far as possible from divine disapproval, he simply took for granted that divinity, much like himself, was capricious and cruel. He no doubt feared the powers that be, but he saw no way of avoiding their attention.

---

25. *Illustrated London News*, Nov. 6, 1937, Colored Plate I.

He was unable to establish the same comfortable connection with divinity the Egyptian enjoyed because the constant threat of change in his environment removed the eternal farther from his reach, and consequently the very threat of the unpredictable (a serious problem for all early peoples), was much more serious here than elsewhere in the Near East. Human desire, of course, strove to dictate to circumstances, to create some lasting bulwark against the caprice of the finite, all with relatively mediocre success. It is easy for us to say he should have learned, after so many rebuffs, to look for causes in phenomena instead of groping blindly around in the supramundane for solutions to problems in his experience; we must not forget that constant fear, engendered by the proximity and immediacy of the unknown, demanded a more swift and certain answer to demanding questions. Fear cowed his heart and at the same time perseverance steeled his resistance and developed the physical equipment necessary to cope with so many obstacles around him. While his emotions directed his petitions, his aspirations to the level of divinity, the pressure of circumstances toughened his skin against the onslaughts of climate and geography.

How did the Mesopotamian conceive of eternity and infinity? Did he have any hope of prolonging the more pleasant aspects of his finite existence into an after-life? Nowhere in his literature do we find the glorified picture of the Ani papyrus; nowhere do we read of a certain promise of improvement. Even Ishtar must submit to the indignities of the lower world and Gilgamesh, for all the glory of his achievements, must share the common lot of all men.[26] This does not mean, however, that man did not enjoy the good things accorded by his experience. The fact that we read more lamentations over the sad blows of fate than lyrical praises from the happy, grateful man simply means that the Mesopotamian, like Job in his misery, felt keenly the deprivation of daily blessings and his inability to account for his loss, while at the same time countless experiences of mis-

---

26. Cf. J. B. Pritchard: *op. cit.,* pp. 88–89.

fortune hardened his resistance without subduing a vague hope
that kept step with the spark of life. Had there been any
correlation between the present life and future rewards, we
should not be surprised to find a disparagement of life, some
sign of asceticism, but of this there is no more indication than
in Egypt. The reason for this attitude toward the infinite lies
in the inability of the subject to lay hands on what was far
removed from the finite or to project his desire into its mirror,
a fact which also prevented him from thinking of the finite as
something morally evil from which he must be cleansed to
attain a perfect good beyond. We get the general impression
that finite experience, in and by itself, was reprehensible largely
because of its tendency to change, frequently to man's disadvantage, for which divine and demonic powers had to assume
their share of responsibility. In spite of so much frustration, man
went on trying, by magic and otherwise, to establish some kind
of link between human desire and an element of security,
regardless of greater uncertainty about the ultimate than in
Egypt, where the line of the pyramid ascended more uncompromisingly to the apex than in the stumbling stages of the
ziggurat. Desire had no more patience with a blank question
than Dante with indifference, and since the Mesopotamian was
uncertain of any form of ultimate happiness, he found it necessary to paint a picture of comparative gloom for the distant
future. Moreover, the instability of the future no doubt caused
him to cling so much more tenaciously to the good things he
found in his present. Such a *Weltanschauung*, in which the
thorn was so sharp behind the rose, gives little quarter to
ecstasy: there was no god to elicit man's full confidence, no
pleasure without the threat of disillusionment. Whatever we
may think of this man's viewpoint, we must admit he was a
character courageous enough to go on reaching out for the
infinite far above and at the same time to make decided advances
on the plane of practice.

In the Near East there was no people so resourceful in
practice as the dweller between the two rivers.[27] We have

----

27. Herodotus (I, 194) was amazed at the river boats made of hides.

already reviewed some of his accomplishments: he built a large network of canals for irrigation; he inaugurated a system of trade and exchange for which he learned how to write binding contracts; he drew up law codes to be consulted as legal reference for all kinds of disputes between citizens; for purposes of war he devised the most effective weapons for offense and defense and laying siege to cities; in architecture, despite a lack of hard stone, he put up structures strong enough to withstand the onslaught of storms and, in many cases, of the enemy as well; he produced a form of writing which became, if not a work of art, the most convenient medium of communication in his day. In all these practical advances, many of which were also developed in Egypt and elsewhere, the Mesopotamian produced something more effective and adequate to prevailing circumstances than others—something more suited to the demands of the changing time and space relations of a finite world. His government, as absolute as we may call it, was a practical one, as natural as the behavior of animals and as arbitrary as the weather. It was to be expected that a group of such people would put their confidence in a ruler of sturdy power who, when he faced divinity, was meek as a lamb, but when he dealt with his subjects or subdued enemies, could be ruthless in his cruelty. His people, of much the same metal, followed him as a flock of sheep after a ram. Thorkild Jacobsen does well to call attention to the similarity between the order in their state and that in the cosmos, between the microcosm and the macrocosm, where united action, in either case, was dictated more by practical expediency than in Egypt where authority in government was supported by a pharaoh of divine descent.[28] The gods would never have thought of crowning Marduk as their champion, had not a crisis, dangerous for all of them, arisen in the form of Tiamat. Compared with the decalogue of the Hebrews, the code of Hammurabi is conspicuous for its down-to-earth, practical common sense. It may seem strange, on the other hand, to learn how practical the Mesopotamian was in reference to

28. *The Intellectual Adventure of Ancient Man,* Chicago, 1946, pp. 127ff.

concrete experience where he depended on trial and error in unpredictable circumstances; it may seem strange to see the same man resort to magic in religion and medicine, relying on a fixed chain of cause and effect relations. Herein lies the greatest inconsistency of his viewpoint.

In spite of the emphasis on practice, there was still a persistent effort on the part of human desire to establish a lasting order which would hold good for practical affairs as well as for the cosmos transcending them, for they believed the former should be dependent on the latter and would no doubt have influenced practice more beneficently, had they been able to penetrate into the ways of the cosmos with more insight. Their failure to establish a common, comprehensive base for these two planes was augmented when magic, the approved method of dealing with the cosmos, was applied to a certain degree in practice, where it functioned as a decided detriment. Reason, whose rudimentary principles they must have been aware of in practice, found it impossible to develop a transcendental dialectic; the imagination created no fanciful utopia beyond life. The writer of the Gilgamesh epic neglected this opportunity in bringing his hero to the abode of Uta-Napishtim; on the other hand, there was an awareness of sin: he knew when he had done wrong, although he was unable, in most cases, to state wherein his offense lay; he knew the gods were angry, but he was not sure they were always righteous in their anger. He was vaguely aware of a difference between what is and what ought to be, without a clear perception of what ought to be. If ever a man saw through a glass darkly into the infinite and eternal or felt himself at a loss to achieve it, it was the Mesopotamian, whether we say he was trying to imitate the cosmos or was completely lost in the transient. Human desire, however, was doing its utmost in both spheres. The Mesopotamian's efforts to maintain order in practical affairs were so serious and time-consuming that life gave him little opportunity to give way to humor, the presence of which implies, among early peoples, some measure of security.

We can also find a number of traces in the cultural expression of Mesopotamia other than the manifestations already mentioned, where we sense the stamp of human desire. In their calendar they wanted the year to conform to the sum of twelve lunar months, but the year refused to submit to such a human calculation (the reason the moon was preferred to the sun as a criterion for astronomical figures was dictated of course, by practical convenience: it was much easier to observe the recurring appearances of the new moon from one month to another than to watch for the next longest or shortest day from one year to another). Number, an artificial creation of human desire, was also imposed on the facts of experience to bring about more order in the transient aspects of living: twelve was a convenient number because it could easily be divided into other even numbers; thirteen was regarded as awkward and therefore unfortunate. Twelve was the number of months in the year, although additions had to be made occasionally to meet the demands of astronomical time. There were also twelve great gods, twelve signs in the zodiac, and twelve divisions in the epic of Gilgamesh.[29] Seven, which also ranked high in their numerology, was hallowed by the number of heavenly bodies, then passes on to nearly all classes of demons, especially those dwelling beneath the earth, and to the gates and walls of the underworld. The number three, which originally must have been associated with the triangle, and four, deriving its importance from the cardinal directions, were not as popular as elsewhere. If we add the fact that every deity was associated with a sacred number and every demon with a fraction, and that the most powerful of all numbers, an unknown one, was in the sole possession of Ea, we cannot escape the conclusion that number itself was divine.

If we look once more at their writing, we find another attempt to achieve permanence, but once more practical contingency cast its shadow, which a practical people could not ignore. Like the Egyptians, their writing reached the hieroglyphic stage, but very soon moved on to a greater compactness and

---

29. Cf. Diodorus, II, 30.

simplification; once the cuneiform became the *lingua franca* of
the Near East, time brought certain deviations and left behind
any attempt at standardization. Ritual was also employed at
religious festivals to keep the motion of the heavenly bodies
and the seasons in a regular, dependable course. Here they
believed they were more successful because their magic was
operating on the plane above practice. The New Year's festival,
the most significant of the year, brought the divinities and
humanity together in a bond of common sympathy, for when
the power of vegetation sank to a low ebb, both god and
man suffered. When the god went into captivity, mankind was
plunged into sorrow and the king, deprived of the insignia of
his office, was exposed to indignities before the statue of the
god; once the king had been restored to his office, the god
emerged from captivity and the whole universe gave itself up
to unbounded rejoicing.[30] All this was an elaborate way of
forcing the most important of all cosmic movements, namely
seasonal change, to follow a regular course for the benefit of
god and man. All these manifestations of subjective desire aiming
at immediate control of circumstances without resorting to a
balanced subject-object relationship in thinking may be listed in
the category of magic. We must also note here the absence of
any word corresponding to the Egyptian ma'at, a term used to
specify the subjective control in the hands of the pharaoh over
the uncertain motions of the finite. In Egypt the divinity of the
monarch was certain of its power to dispense this justice or
order, but in Mesopotamia, where the connection between god
and man was far less certain, magic of another sort had to
serve as a substitute.[31] Yes, there were law codes, but law,
while it was practical and maintained some kind of order in
society, could not control the world at large. In Egypt, magic,
among other things, was apparently concerned with reassuring
the subject in his own certainty, while in Mesopotamia it was
forever groping in the mysterious beyond in many directions;

30. For a description of the New Year's festival consult H. Frankfort:
Kingship and the Gods, Chicago, 1948, pp. 318ff.
31. H. Frankfort: *op. cit.*, p. 262.

the individual could not be too sure of his certainty. In medicine, too, magic was especially strong, perhaps because the Mesopotamian thought of disease as something beyond practical control.[32]

We must be careful when we say there was a completely parallel relation between the Mesopotamian's view of the cosmos and the structure of his society and government, because he was not able to control the gods as he wished and the methods he applied to the control of divinity, on the one hand, and of practical affairs, on the other, were not always the same. It is true that he created gods that reflected, in their dealings with men and each other, something of the unscruplous behavior of cosmic forces, that the functioning of society and government carried this analogy even further, but his attitude toward the powers that be and his more common-sense way of dealing with practical problems resulted in two different modes of thinking, a difference more obvious in this culture where man coped with the finite on one plane and then attempted to deal with the infinite on another. The emphasis on magic points to a prevailing fear of cosmic forces, which prevented him from applying to the cosmos at large the thought processes he had learned to use in practice.

As we have seen, the Egyptian, in addition to the divinity of the monarch and his magic, sought for some common denominator by which he could control the fickle transiency of experience and bring human desire to a closer identification with the infinite; this he accomplished by reducing haphazard limitations to the static, geometric line. Did the Mesopotamian, in spite of the uncertainty of his connection with the infinite, and involved as he was in the maelstrom of practical experience—did he ever discover such a common denominator to render his position more secure? The more common to all the phases of his life, the nearer this attribute would bring him to the security of the infinite.

What the Egyptian found in the geometric line the Mesopo-

---

32. Herodotus (I, 197) tells us they had no physicians.

tamian discovered in the expression of power. It was first called
forth by the climate and environment of his homeland. It
produced powerful men capable of overcoming great obstacles;
it helped to produce many of the cultural advances of the
Sumerians; it protected them against their enemies. If the static
can be called the burden of the Nile valley, much the same can
be said for power on the Euphrates. What originally was merely
a means to social and cultural ends eventually became a desired
end in itself and thus checked any further advance in several
directions. While the early Sumerians were struggling against
great odds, such an emphasis was a boon to their cause, but
when the Assyrian empire was established with poor natural
barriers, the people had little time for anything except keeping
the empire intact by fighting off the enemy and gathering in the
booty. As long as the economy of the land supported this program, as long as native soldiers were at hand, the Assyrian
gloried in his wide-spread expression of power; once decay
gnawed from within, the collapse was as devastating as it was
sudden. There was no more effective way of dealing with these
people than by using force and, like Hitler and Mussolini, they
showed respect only for the enemy who opposed them on their
own terms. They seemed to enjoy thoroughly the physical
experience of overcoming an obstacle, not so much for the gain
involved as for a kind of somatic catharsis. They were doers of
the word; like most animals, they tried to solve many of their
problems by aggressive action. Gilgamesh was more than a
little distressed because death was a problem he could not
conquer by physical prowess, and mentally he had very little
equipment to cope with it. As is so frequently the case among
people of superior physical development, the bold, aggressive
front is a cloak for some deep-seated fear; in the dark one cries
aloud and engages in shadow boxing to conceal his fear from
himself.

In general, the divinities of Mesopotamia gave expression to
moods of ruthlessness, especially Enlil, who descended with
wind, rain, and flood upon a defenseless humanity; he gives no
evidence of the "quality of mercy." In the epic the character

of Gilgamesh is the most representative of his people, dealing with subjects as if they were so many mechanical slaves, and if he defends them against an enemy, he thinks only of his own satisfaction in so doing; he slays one monster after another for the sake of physical adventure; he shows little respect for the gods; in fact, he bows before nothing but death, which threatens to rob him of his physical power. He and Adapa, who breaks the wing of the wind, are both creatures of will, a will to act without giving quarter to reflection. Naturally, the man of the street realized he could not follow such an example in business contracts or social relationships, but in war, where disguise for the sake of expediency was cast off, he showed no consideration for the enemy; not only the leader or king, but every soldier is represented as dealing out cruel destruction on his opponent. When the Assyrian monarch was not on the warpath, he expended his energies in hunting the wild beast, again making a display of power against power. The *lex talionis,* which saturates the legal codes of Mesopotamia, prescribed the punishment meted out by the strong man upon a culprit who became an instrument for his expression of power, a procedure meeting with approval in a society of strong men. If we compare the accounts of the historical battles of Egypt with the sculptured reliefs showing the pharaoh overpowering his enemies with the greatest ease, we must supply some divine agency working in and through the latter to enable him, in spite of his size, to accomplish such feats; let us then compare the accounts of Sennacherib and Esarhaddon with sculptured reproductions and we shall understand how the former, relying on their physical power as represented, could credibly catch a number of enemies in a net and then impale them.[33] Up to the time of Gudea this surging power is still a means to an end, but for the Assyrians the strength of cords and muscles, encased in triple steel, is almost an end in itself. The walls and towers of their cities present fearful bulwarks of power in the face of any opposition. Is it any wonder that any further cultural development bogged

---

33. J. B. Pritchard: *op. cit.,* pp. 287ff.

down under the pressure of such an incubus? They were willing, however, to pay such a price for subjective security and satisfaction which, in both Egypt and Mesopotamia, exerted much the same effect as the wall of convention and the roof of perfection in China.

It requires no great amount of discrimination to realize the Mesopotamian fits pretty well into Sheldon's category of the somatotonic temperament, whatever we may think of such categories.[34] We have already mentioned the difficulty of estimating personality traits of early peoples because they cannot be brought into the modern laboratory, but a comparison of somatotonic traits with what we have already observed in this chapter reveals some striking similarities. These include, first of all, an assertiveness of body posture and movement, then a preference for physical adventure of all kinds, a wealth of energy, and craving for physical exercise. A cursory examination of Assyrian reliefs will reveal these predominant traits in the pursuits of both war and the hunt. The dictatorial lust for domination over others and the methods employed to keep people under the Mesopotamian's control were inspired by the notion that authority can best be maintained when backed up by force.[35] Physical fearlessness, another trait, we cannot deny the Mesopotamian; he was also ruthless in being purposely cruel to the extent that—and this applies especially to the Assyrian— he seems to have enjoyed it for its own sake. What Sheldon calls a "horizontal mental cleavage" (*loc. cit.*, p. 64) comes out in the separation between the bold and practical face he turned to the objective world and his superstitious approach to the unpredictable divinity, which means he was the ancient counterpart of the modern bully, cloaking his fears in boisterous, aggressive action. There is no indication of a retreat within for the sake of self-recreation, if we can rely on the objective obviousness of his pleasures, his bare-faced approach when compared with

---

34. W. H. Sheldon: *The Varieties of Temperament*, New York, 1942, pp. 49ff.

35. Cf. T. Jacobsen: *The Intellectual Adventure of Ancient Man*, Chicago, 1946, p. 143.

the Egyptian and the Hindu. Once he found himself in a situation where direct action was of no avail, he, like Gilgamesh, raised a great hue and cry but never fell back on solitude or sentimentality; in dealing with others, he remained consistently the same man so that all comers knew exactly what to expect of him; thus the man of action avoided too many doubts, absent-minded quandaries and also ignored the disturbing paradoxes of the mind that arise from a conflict of theory and practice.

There was, then, a dichotomy between the level of horizontal, more objective experience which the Mesopotamian sought to control by his strength, and the level of divinity of which he stood in awe. Human desire was as concentrated in Mesopotamia as elsewhere, and when magic was given a free hand it was bound to thwart a balanced subject-object relation in thinking. We have seen this tendency at work in his use of sacred numbers and other symbols, but in the fields of law and business, where finite change made obvious demands, he saw and dealt with the object much more clearly. We do not claim that law and business show no signs of magic; nor are they free from the expression of power, but they do reveal an attempt to be fair to two opposing parties, which requires some kind of a balance between subject and object from the most expedient of men. For this fact we should be thankful that the monarch was not a divinity endowed with final authority to pass, directly or indirectly, on such subjects. Another advance, also resulting from this dichotomy, came in the awareness of tragedy and its meaning, especially in the Gilgamesh epic, although the concept was not fully developed. Had there been a solid, connecting link between the levels of the human and the divine, had the ways of god been more open and accessible to man's curiosity and desire, magic would have forced divinity to comply more completely with man's longing for future security, for clear revelation, which in turn had to be interpreted by the priesthood. An atmosphere of tragedy has no room in a scheme of things where certainty can have its own way.

At this point we shall do well to make a clearer comparison of the Mesopotamian with the Egyptian: on the Nile and on the

Euphrates the demands of daily subsistence brought about certain improvements which must have called for common-sense reasoning, although we cannot expect to learn much about the thought processes leading up to irrigation, tilling of the soil, building, etc., because the ancient was never conscious of the mental steps in his thinking. There was another sphere above which subjective desire, in Egypt, was able to convert into an infinite haven of security, and this was brought into a close rapport with finite experience by magic, by the use of the static line and, above all, by the power of a divine pharaoh. So effectively was the finite hemmed in by the hard and fast rules of convention, dictated by absolute authority, it is difficult for us to see where one leaves off and the other begins. In Mesopotamia the climate and geography brought forth more change, which was responsible for more common-sense thinking in practice and made it more difficult to make the cosmos and its divinities subservient to man's desire for permanence, especially since the monarch had little control over it. Man was therefore uncertain about his standing with divinity and the margin of difference between the two spheres was more pronounced; nor was he able to put aside his fear of uncertainty long enough to face squarely the problem of the unknown; furthermore, the problem would not yield to the force of physical action which had spelled a certain amount of success in practice. Had the Mesopotamian been able to dispense with a porthole looking out to the infinite and the priest with his domineering revelation, he could have discovered the value of theory in a scientific viewpoint, where theory must be stripped of its sacrosanct and stereotyped character. This advance would have brought him nearer to the outlook of the later Greek.

The element of uncertainty he attacked in two different ways; in other words, he sought for truth along two different avenues of investigation. The knowledge he gained from practical experience, which we may call scientific in a rudimentary sense, ran closely parallel with its application. His theory of law can be summed up in terms of action: "If you do so and so, so and so shall be done to you," and it is difficult to think of the

Mesopotamian theorizing any further about law or legal procedure. Had someone asked him how to make a vase, his explanation would have been most effective by way of practical demonstration. In his own way he must have known something about definition and comparison; however, his fear of the cosmos at large hemmed in his imagination and prevented the extension of a balanced subject-object relation so necessary for the development of scientific theory. On the plane of the divine, knowledge was tantamount to revelation, coming down from authority to satisfy the subject's greed for certainty. The dictum that "the fear of the Lord is the beginning of wisdom" kept the heart and head raised to the fountain of divination from which no amount of persuasion could have turned him aside, although the certainty he derived from authority was by no means as consoling as in Egypt. Had someone urged him to tap another source of information, the Mesopotamian would have been at a loss to use it; his attitude was like that of a man who reads in several articles that smoking is bad for his health and therefore stops reading altogether. Although divinity was not so easily controlled by man, divination was theoretically impeccable, even if at times frustrating in its results.

The government of this people we should call an absolute monarchy whose ruler controlled all domestic and foreign policy with an iron hand, but because his office was definitely bound up with the priesthood without enjoying divine descent, his position, from one angle, was rather precarious compared with that of the Egyptian ruler. The monarch was a symbol of the two worlds the Mesopotamian tried to reconcile in his viewpoint. The diorite statue of Gudea affords ample testimony to the power with which the monarch wished to impress his subject; the stele of Hammurabi, presenting the humble ruler before the god of justice, shows how he looked up to the powers of the cosmos. The king, in his code, plays the role of a steward; he enumerates all the blessings he has bestowed on his people, all the favors he has offered to his god; later he becomes a demon of power when he curses the man who dares to mar any part of the code. Government was in a somewhat compromising position between the realms of the known and unknown, the religious and the secular, between common-sense knowledge and revelation. While the ruler, because he was not a divine descendant, had no right to exercise as much arbitrary authority as the pharaoh, he still prevented, because of the weight of religion pressing down upon his office, the common-sense viewpoint of experience from gaining access to the unknown of the cosmos and from achieving a victory over revelation. The ruler of Egypt was a standing guarantee that the infinite would continue to reflect itself into and frame itself around the finite so that the fine line separating the two was most deceptive; the ruler of Mesopotamia had to exert all his strength to preserve an unstable connection between two obviously separated and unrelated aspects of man's world.

The moral side of the picture reveals no improvement over Egypt because of a failure to develop anything like a center of moral responsibility within man himself. Magic, with its emphasis on subjective power, was substituted for self-responsibility and frequently destroyed the possibility of fair treatment for the object. Right and wrong, which ought to be determined by individual judgment, were then made subordinate to subjective means and power expressed in terms of action. The relations between divinities gave no quarter to a sense of moral responsibility, and when the gods abandoned a ruler and his city, there was no choice for the citizen but to follow suit; otherwise the people followed the monarch whom the gods had blessed with power. When respect for an object failed, which invariably happened in the absence of self-responsibility, the subject resorted to expediency, a procedure which hallows the means to the detriment of the end or object, and this was the most effective means the Mesopotamian found at his disposal, especially for controlling the powers above man's level. On the plane of practice, expediency has a parallel in the dictum that might makes right, and this the Mesopotamian was not slow in applying, whenever possible, to the sphere of action. The initial move to undermine magic in favor of moral integrity had to wait for encouragement from another quarter.

Art achieved no more independence here than on the banks

of the Nile. Like any object in the hands of an all-powerful subject, it served as a convenient tool for the demonstration of power: whether in color or stone it enhanced the glory of the monarch, guarded the palace, recorded the exploits of war and hunt, furnished authority with a seal, and entered into the service of magic. The artist, his identity completely submerged, was a mouthpiece for authority in the guise of both state and religion. As in Egypt, there was probably a feeling for decorative art and its use of color and design, but beyond this suggestion the Mesopotamian artist could do little or nothing for his art, except to mold it into a general expression of the people's viewpoint.

Egypt defied the relativity of time and space and overcame its fear of change by creating the most integrated expression of human striving to furnish man with a consummate self-identification with the infinite. For her success, which may be accounted as either a great achievement, burden, or illusion, she had to pay a high price. The Mesopotamian was at a loss to forge a satisfactory connecting link between himself and the heavens above and therefore relied more on magic and the strong man of action to serve his purpose on this side of the grave.

What, then, is the nature of human desire that sought and still seeks to transcend the world of the here and now in favor of something different from human experience? Why attempt to eternalize the finite or bludgeon every opposing obstacle into the submission of comparative dependability and security? Plato was the first thinker to essay an answer to these questions, and whatever we may think of his contribution, we cannot claim to have penetrated any deeper. Why should there be such a paradox of the finite and infinite? We can merely say it has given birth to what we call problems, whether we are conscious of them or not, and in struggling with problems the mind and body have grown to be more effective and proficient. Beyond this point we can only point to the ultimate and be patient. We can see the implications and contradictions implicit in such a paradox, but we are still groping for the fundamental reasons for it as much as the ancient Mesopotamian.